YOUNG AND DRIVEN

*A GUIDE TO MAKING YOUR DREAMS
COME TRUE FOR THE YOUNG AND
YOUNG AT HEART*

BY

DR. CORTLAN J. WICKLIFF, ESQ.

For the men and women that presented me consistently high benchmarks to achieve. Thank you for being the giants on whose shoulders I stand. Every day I strive towards the standards you set before me.

Table of Contents

Foreword

My eyes still well up as I recall the tragedy that drove my son to become Dr. Cortlan James Wickliff, Esq.

I sat in the living room waiting on my son Cortlan to come home from school asking myself, "How do you communicate extremely devastating news to a 10-year-old child?" Amid my numbness and excruciating pain, as the author of this book walked through the door after school that dreadful afternoon in October of 2000, that is exactly what I had to do. Unsuccessfully straining to hold back tears, I managed to utter the unthinkable. "Your dad died last night from a heart attack in his sleep…"

That was the longest-short conversation I had ever had. He didn't really ask many questions, break down crying, or react with the disbelief or confusion I had expected. Instead, he said, "I better go tell coach I won't be at practice for a bit," and he immediately walked out the door. Did he understand what had just happened? Was he in shock? That was a dark day. However, what happens in the next few days is nothing short of amazing and I believe divinely orchestrated.

But first a little about Cortlan... Anybody who hears his story invariably wants to know, "when did you know he was different."

His dad and I discovered that we had a unique child, back in the beginning of the summer of 1994, when he was 3yrs old. That summer, like we did most summers, we brought several of our nieces and nephews to stay with us and participate in local summer programs. This particular year, I was a bit overzealous. I somehow piled 7 or more kids in my little Geo Metro and made the 4-hour-trip from Liberty, Texas to our home in Austin. Seeing the clown-car like scene of all those people getting out of a vehicle barely bigger than a Toyota Prius, made Tony (Cortlan's dad) decide we needed to have a family meeting. During this meeting, his dad discussed the schedule for household chores with his older two brothers and I.

As the meeting ended, Tony reiterated the assignment of chores and expectations of everyone in our home. The only person he did not directly address was 3-year-old Cortlan. Tony then ended the meeting, so he thought, with a pair of questions.

Tony: **Do you all understand? Does anyone have anything to say?**

After an extended silence, the smallest person in the room boldly proclaimed in his full voice:

Cortlan: **Yes, daddy. If no one else has anything to say, I have something to say.**

Surprised to receive any feedback, let alone feedback from his youngest son, Tony asked him what he wanted to say.

Cortlan replied, "The way I see it, daddy, it sounds like you are ready to be the boss of the house now and if you are ready to be the boss, you need to do things for yourself..."

We were stunned. His brothers were terrified, his dad was irritated, and his cousins in the next room got extremely quiet. If it had stopped there, it would have been enough. But Tony, being a mix of irritated and curious asked, "Is there anything else."

Cortlan gladly volunteered specifics oblivious to how irritated the man sitting next to him was becoming. Cortlan proceeded to tell his father that he should not request his children to get things like his ash tray or cigarettes, but get them himself. Despite Tony turning a brighter shade of red by the second, he kept asking Cortlan for more. "And the way I see it, the boss should pay the bills, too."

Angrily Tony inquired, "Since you know so much, what do you suggest that I pay?"

Boldly and naively Cortlan continued, "The way I see it, if mom pays the house bill, you can pay my school bill; and if mom pays the light bill, you can pay the 'sink' bill." The phrase "sink-bill" reminded everyone in the house that Cortlan was only 3 years old. In that moment, my nieces and nephews in the next room erupted in laughter, Cortlan's brothers let out some giggles, and even I chuckled a bit.

Nevertheless, Tony was not distracted by the laughter, and Cortlan didn't get the joke. Tony undeterred, stone-faced, and red with anger asked if there was anything else. Completely oblivious to the danger he was in, Cortlan, yet again said, "The way I see it..."

Before he could utter another word, I took the chaotic laughter as a nice break to stop the conversation and send all the kids outside to play.

Tony was convinced that I had put Cortlan up to saying all of those things, or that he was repeating something that I had said. I, of course, had nothing to do with Cortlan's expressed opinion. Back then people could only pay bills by mail or in person. There was no online option. Thus, whenever I had a bill to pay, I would pay them while taking Cortlan to and from school each day. Like most kids his age, Cortlan asked a lot of questions, and I answered them. I recall inquiries like:

"What are you doing mommy?" I replied, "I am mailing the mortgage payment for our house."

"Why?" I responded, "When you are an adult you have to pay bills." –Or–

He asked, "Mommy, what's that piece of paper?" "It's a check to pay for your school." etc.

After Cortlan's exchange with Tony, I realized that while running errands and entertaining the curious questions of my toddler son, Cortlan had been observing and drawing conclusions of his own. This level of deductive reasoning was well beyond the scope of a typical child his age. Because of that fact, it was utterly impossible trying to convince my husband that I had nothing to do with it. This meant that Tony spent the entire summer thinking I was trying to "poison his son against him."

Though the rest of the summer was a bit awkward in our home, early in the fall semester I would be exonerated.

His dad soon found out for himself just how inquisitive and 'helpful' Cortlan could be. In the fall, Cortlan was 4 years old and starting Pre-Kindergarten school. Tony decided that, instead of paying for afterschool daycare, he would watch Cortlan at his auto-body and paint shop in the afternoons. This would have been a great way to save money if Tony had lasted more than a week.

A few days into the first week of school, I received a call from Tony. "Come get Cortlan as soon as possible!"

I frantically asked what was wrong. In that moment my mind was flooded with the horrible images of our 4-year-old having hurt himself with one of my husband's industrial tools. Tony, oblivious to my fears, went on to say that Cortlan had taken it upon himself to organize the tool

4

area in the shop, stating safety concerns; he had also prepared a phone script for the receptionist answering the phone to better give customer updates. Tony said that he was generally trying to run his business! His employees got a big laugh out of the whole situation because, per them, Cortlan was actually doing a good job. This meant that Tony was on the receiving end of several jokes about his son running the business better than he did. Needless to say, Tony gladly paid for afterschool care from that point on.

Despite an occasional, unique, uncharacteristic event like the few mentioned above, Cortlan displayed otherwise very normal child-like behavior. He played soccer, liked his chemistry set, loved movies and enjoyed playing with his family and friends. However, he did seem to always be thinking and analyzing even when he wasn't sharing his thoughts. So, in October of 2000 when his dad died, I was very concerned about how this might affect him. On the day of his dad's funeral, I got my first glimpse of the impact Tony's untimely death would have on Cortlan.

We were midway through the funeral and had just concluded the portion of the program whereby several people had shared fond memories and expressed words of comfort to the family. I was in such pain; I just wanted it to be over. The preacher was at the lectern preparing to share the scripture for the eulogy when Cortlan stood up and walked to the microphone that was still located near his father's coffin. I guess Cortlan had thought about giving expressions but as a child attending his first funeral, he did not realize that we had proceeded pass that portion of the program. The preacher, however, was gracious and yielded the floor to Cortlan. Many of us were in shock and had no idea what to expect as Cortlan had never spoken in such a public event. What did a child have to say, especially on an occasion such as this? He cleared his throat and with his voice a bit shaky he began to speak.

"Hello everyone. My name is Cortlan Wickliff. I am 10 years old and I am the youngest child of Tony Wickliff. I was sitting there thinking about everything. I still can hardly believe that this is real. I wish it wasn't. I keep waiting on him to sit up in the casket and start laughing at all of us for having these sad faces. I really learned a lot from my dad, including how to be strong – mostly from him joking and picking with me." Since the audience knew Tony's character as a fun-loving jokester, that statement provoked the audience to release a loud laugh that seemed to relax Cortlan a bit. He continued. *"God is a good God and He would not have taken my dad unless my dad had done all that God wanted him to do here on earth. Since my dad obviously completed his purpose for being here, God took him on to heaven. Now it is all of our responsibilities to do the same. We have to find out what is our God given purpose and then make sure that we get busy doing it so we can fulfill our purpose too like my dad did, before God calls us home. Thank you."*

There was not a dry eye in the packed church as everyone rushed to their feet and gave a standing ovation that seemed to last for several minutes. Cortlan had spoken in church and recited prewritten speeches in school. I call this his first public speech because this was the first time he stood up and delivered his own words un-coached and unassisted. And for the majority of the family, it was their first time seeing what his father and I had learned 6 years earlier; there was something unique about him.

For Cortlan, I believe it was his public declaration of the start of a journey to live a purpose driven life. Soon afterward, he shared with me the positive impact that he planned to have on society. He would start that journey by achieving those seemingly farfetched academic goals he had set years earlier. This time, though, there was something different about the way he said it.

He began to set short-term goals, get focused, develop plans, follow them and achieve each goal. Then he would set another goal, achieve it and repeat. He allowed the tragedy of his father's death to chart a trajectory for his journey that has already resulted in historic achievements.

This book contains a roadmap of how he did it. Honestly, it was sometimes challenging to be the type of supportive parent that Cortlan required. For instance, when

 he was accepted to college at age 14, he had to move 250 miles away from home into the university dorm only a week after his 15th birthday. I learned how to encourage, pray and be a voice of reason for him, sometimes all in the same conversation. Above all, I was always his parent first, even from a distance. His journey required me to suppress my fears and worries often, to help him mature and grow through his challenges. More about that in the next book…

For now, as his mother and now a professional peer, his achievements in spite of very difficult and seemingly unfair obstacles are an inspiration to me. Hopefully, after you learn more about his journey in this book, you will be inspired to pursue and achieve your dreams too.

Congratulations Cortlan, I love you!

Your proud Mom,

Dr. Tanya Dugat Wickliff,
Professor of Engineering Practice
College of Engineering at Texas A&M University

Prologue

The title "<u>Young and Driven</u>," has two very important connections to my life.

The first reason for the title is the more straightforward interpretation of the title. It is meant to be a play on the phrase "Young & Dumb." This is actually a phrase that came up during my orientation at Harvard Law School.

Law school orientation was a daunting experience, to say the least. You are gathered in a room with over 500 new students. Then we were told how successful everyone is; your classmates are Hollywood actors, business owners, Olympians, Rhodes Scholars, hedge fund managers, and the list goes on. The entire experience was intimidating, and largely a blur. Nevertheless, I distinctly remember one thing that was said.

Most of the time was spent encouraging and congratulating us on our accomplishments thus far. In the midst of that canned praise, we got one word of warning, "No matter what you do from here on, you will never again be able to say that you were young and dumb."

Considering that we were starting law school and, on average, the members of the audience was about 24-25 years old, had at least one college degree, and had worked for 1-2 years, this was a reasonable statement to make. However, I personally took exception to that statement. I was barely 20 years old. It didn't seem fair that less than 3 weeks out of my teens, I no longer could have young and dumb moments. It seemed like I was being deprived of a rite of passage.

Yet, the more I thought about it, the better I felt. What does it mean to be young and dumb? It means to exist in a phase of life where you do not know what you want from life and/or how to get it. When you are young, you do reckless and illogical things, but not because you strive to be illogical. You act in objectively illogical and reckless manners because you are pursuing the wrong goals or pursuing the right goals in the wrong manner.

Thus, being young and dumb means prioritizing short-term gains at the expense of long-term success. With that understanding, I realized that I never want to be that kind of person. And for the majority of my life, I had not been that person. I knew what I wanted and systematically moved towards my goals.

This doesn't mean that I never made mistakes, or that I never did stuff that I later realized was idiotic. Throughout this book, you will see examples of these naïve moments and bone-head mistakes. Success is not the absence of failure, but the perseverance over it.

Have you heard the adage: "Make a mistake once and it becomes a lesson; make the same mistake twice and it becomes a choice."

Well, I live by a similar creed, "See or make a mistake once and it becomes a lesson; afterward, make that same mistake and it becomes a choice." It is my hope that you can see the mistakes that I made, and use them as lessons to make your journey easier.

If not young and dumb; what should you be? For me, the answer has been driven! One of the benefits of being young is everything is possible because you haven't learned any differently. I am defined by my desire to pursue and achieve my "impossible" dreams regardless of what stands in my way. It is my hope that, regardless of your age, you will hold onto this kind of youthful resolve and let it drive you to do extraordinary things.

The second reason for the title is a personal one. My dad was a mechanic all of my life; as a result, my time with him was inextricably linked to cars. Whether it was him teaching me how to use a buffer, us doing donuts in an old Cadillac he was fixing, or racing go-karts on the dirt road in front of his shop, to be around dad was to be around cars. Perhaps my earliest memory was sitting in his lap "steering" his truck up Parmer Lane on the way to our house. I put "steering" in quotes because I would hope he didn't let a 3-4year old kid actually take complete control of the wheel. Although, with Dad, there is no telling.

My dad has been a central motivating force for most of the achievements I have made thus far and continues to inspire and motivate me to this day. So it seems fitting that the title of this book should have something to do with cars. Thus, the title <u>Young and Driven</u> pays homage to the man who both taught me how to drive and be driven.

Despite the title, this book will not be rife with driving analogies. I do not live my life a quarter-mile at a time, and road trips did not teach me everything I need to know about life. The central theme of this book is: *Success can be achieved by anyone who is driven enough to apply unrelenting, consistent, and intentional effort to make their dreams a reality.*

Chapter 1:
Introduction: Driven to Achieve

A 3rd-grade kid does a book report on Dr. Martin Luther King Jr. and is filled with excitement because he found out something he had never heard before. This elementary age kid finds out that Dr. King got his Ph.D. when he was 26 years old. He is so excited that he tells you that he is going to get a doctorate degree just like Dr. King. He adds that he is going to get his doctorate before he turns 26 years old. What do you say to him? Kids do say the darndest things, so maybe you write it off the first time.

However, what do you say a year later when this kid still has it in his mind that he is going to graduate with a doctorate degree by his 26th birthday and has now picked his majors? He proudly announces that he plans to get a B.S. in some kind of engineering, a law degree, and then maybe find an M.D. / Ph.D. program to finally achieve his title as Doctor. Do you tell him that he can't do it? That might be too harsh. Instead, do you just let him know that in order to accomplish this goal he would have to start college no later than the age of 15?

What do you say six years later when, at the age of 14, he is actually applying to college? How would you advise him five years after that, when he is graduating with his B.S. in Bioengineering from Rice University at the age of 19? Now he is the youngest engineer in the nation, but still pushing towards a bigger dream; would you think it was possible? Would you be convinced three years after that when he graduates from Harvard Law School with his J.D. at the age of 22 as one of the youngest black law school graduates in the school's more than 200-year history? Do you know what you would say six months later when he is admitted to the Texas State bar as the youngest of more than 94,000 attorneys in the state while completing his first semester in a Ph.D. program? Can you imagine the elation he felt 2 ½ years after that when he is only 26 days away from receiving his Ph.D. in Engineering, and 30 days away from his 26th birthday? Was that hard to imagine?

I am that kid! Starting in the 3rd grade, I spent almost 20 years working towards the same goal; I was going to become Dr. Wickliff at a younger age than Dr. King graduated with his doctorate. During the pursuit of my goal, I have been called a dreamer, unrealistic, naïve, immature, uninformed, ignorant, childish, and a lot of other synonyms that I tried to forget. This name calling came from all different directions; it came from people who were old, young, near-and-dear, and relative strangers. Some of the discouragement was even well-intentioned. They were trying to get me to realize that I was pursuing what they believed to be an unattainable pipe dream. It would be a lie to tell you that I didn't spend several nights lying awake thinking the same thing, especially during the difficult times. However, less than a month away from achieving what many thought was unachievable, a dream that has been 18 years in the making, people finally stopped telling me how impossible my dream was. Eventually, people started asking me how and why I did it.

When asked why I have given a lot of reasons – I wanted the title doctor, I wanted to have as many career options as possible, I am genuinely interested in all of my chosen fields, I want to be qualified for jobs with high levels of responsibility, etc. All of which are true. Yet, none of those reasons are what got me through 11 years of all-nighters in college, or years of early morning meetings and late work days. Although I have always been greatly inspired by the example of Dr. King, my greatest motivation was given to me by another man in October of 2000.

I did not know it at the time, but early that month I would have my last face to face conversation with my dad, Anthony "Tony" Wickliff. I remember vividly coming outside of my family's church in Liberty, TX to see my dad standing, leaning over his pickup truck. We talked a bit about school and then, out of nowhere, he said,

"Son, when you get rich and famous, I only want one thing."

"Of course dad, what is it?"

He responded, "Buy me a Corvette."

My dad had been a mechanic for most of my life; it wasn't just his occupation, it was his true passion. He had worked his way up from a volunteer to the owner of his own auto body, paint, and mechanic shop. His hands and forearms were always a few shades darker than the rest of his body from engine grease that just never seemed to disappear. In fact, he seemed to have oil stains on everything that he owned, from his jeans and t-shirts to his Sunday best. This was because there was never a time when he wouldn't fix a car for someone, which, on more than one occasion, included resurrecting a car in a church parking lot. As such, I am thankful that he never had to find out how little his 10-year-old son knew about cars, because I think I would have made him feel somewhat embarrassed. When he asked me for a Corvette, I had no idea what it was. So I naively responded, "How about I get you a Ferrari or a…"

Before I could finish the sentence to suggest a Hummer, Range Rover, or some other car I had seen in a movie, dad interrupted me and said, "Stop acting like your mom, always trying to tell me what's best for me." He chuckled in his comical, unique way and declared, "I want a Corvette."

In that moment, I promised my dad that I would become successful enough to buy him a new Corvette. Because I had never seen the sticker price of his dream car, I had no idea the level of success I was committing to achieve.

That promise stuck with me, because, less than a week later, my dad died from a heart attack. Just as vividly as I remember my dad leaning over his pickup truck asking me for a Corvette, I remember opening my front door to find my mom standing in the middle of the living room crying when I got home from school. There are few things more devastating to anyone, let alone a 10-year-old boy, than talking to someone that you love before going to bed, and finding out he died a few hours later in his sleep. One of those things, that did hurt worse, was finding out, he went to the doctor to get checked out earlier that month but couldn't afford any of the diagnostic and preventative care that might have saved his life. That kind of hurt never fully goes away, but if you work at it, you can find a way to let it drive you. And that is what I did.

See the more I learned about Corvettes, the more I realized the level of faith that my dad had placed in me. Dad was from a farming/ranching family and was raised on handshake deals and cash businesses. This meant that every automobile part he ordered, every tool he owned, and every car he bought was with cash. One day while reflecting on my dad's death, it dawned on me that, in his mind, he fully expected that his 10-year-old son was going to become the type of man who would someday be able to buy him a brand new Corvette – in cash. Wow!

Why he thought that and what he was expecting me to accomplish, I will never know. The best I could figure is that he must have believed that naïve 3rd grader who had told him these outlandish dreams 3 years earlier. If that is the case, then he fully expected that the type of person who could pull that off would be able to get him his dream car. So, it became my personal mission to live up to the potential that Dad saw in me. However, it wasn't just to make my dad proud, or to one day be able to own an excellent piece of American muscle in honor of him; although, those were definitely motivators. More importantly, I want to become the type of man he expected because that kind of man would have the ability to take care of the people that I care about. I could help ensure that those people could have access to the medical care that they need, and I would never have to bury a loved one for the need of a few extra dollars.

I know that I have not yet fully become the person that I believe Dad expected me to become, but in 26 days, as I write this book, I will be one giant step closer.

This chapter has shown you a bit about what ignited the drive to achieve academically within me. It is my sincere belief and experience that: *Success can be achieved by anyone who is driven enough to apply unrelenting, consistent, and intentional effort to make their dreams a reality*. The question becomes "How?" How did I turn my drive into achievement, and more importantly how can you? That question is what this book will address.

Although I will share stories and experiences from my life, this is not an autobiography. This book will present the concrete steps that I took and would recommend for anybody trying to pursue an ambitious dream. Though I have applied them, thus far, to academic pursuits and career goals, they can be applied to any dream – whether you are pursuing academic excellence, success on your job, team achievement, a new career, or taking that first leap into entrepreneurship. Thus, journey with me in the pages that follow and you too can build lasting accomplishment and make your dreams come true.

Chapter 2:
Believe

All great accomplishments start with your belief, and that is where we will start.

Regardless of what dream you are pursuing, achieving any major accomplishment in life is like constructing a new building. Any great building starts with some great groundwork. Before you can lay a foundation or put up a frame, you have to have a ground that is suitable to build on.

Belief is the ground on which the foundation for achievement can be laid. Matthew 7:24-27 says "Therefore everyone who hears these words of mine and puts them into practice is like a wise man who built his house on the rock. The rain came down, the streams rose, and the winds blew and beat against that house; yet it did not fall, because it had its foundation on the rock. But everyone who hears these words of mine and does not put them into practice is like a foolish man who built his house on sand. The rain came down, the streams rose, and the winds blew and beat against that house, and it fell with a great crash."

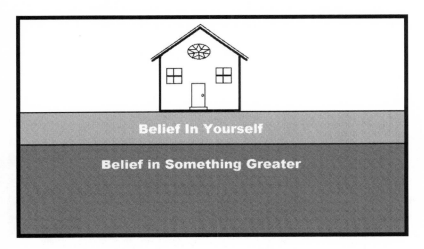

I use this parable to illustrate the idea that belief is more fundamental than the foundation. Belief is the solid ground that anchors your efforts against adversity. If you do not believe in what you are doing or believe that your accomplishments are possible, then when the storms of life approach, your efforts will crumble and you will give up. Therefore, without solid belief, you will never be able to build towards a significant accomplishment.

As in the parable, imagine building a structure. Underneath that structure is your belief. Much like the ground has multiple layers, so too does your belief. There are two primary levels of belief that are paramount for success: belief in yourself which is the ground closest to the surface, and belief in something greater than yourself which makes up the deeper bedrock.

We will start with the surface (i.e. belief in yourself). No matter how strong and resilient the bedrock you build on is, if you do not have solid ground above it, your foundation can be shifted. Similarly, no matter how deep your faith is in something greater than yourself (e.g. family, God, country, laws, karma, etc.), a solid belief in yourself is still paramount for building any lasting accomplishments.

Belief In Something Greater

Belief in yourself is often the hardest part of anyone's journey, and in several areas of your life, it will become a daily struggle. The fact of the matter is, despite all of the songs, memes, parables and popular culture that tell us to "shake [our] haters off," often times you are your own biggest nay-sayer. You will tell yourself you can't accomplish a goal before you ever hear it from someone else. There is no way that you will be successful if that continues.

"Believe in yourself!" This is easy to say but hard to do. The first step in the process is to stop putting other people on a pedestal. Often, the reason you don't believe in yourself is because you elevate people above you. We look at other people as having some "it-factor" that we lack, or

> "I was never top of the class at school, but my classmates must have seen potential in me, because my nickname was 'Einstein'"
> Dr. Stephen Hawking

some understanding of the world we don't get. Instead of saying that somebody did better than you on a test because they studied harder, or a teammate beat you out for a starting position because they trained harder, our first assumption is that they are smarter or better than we are. Realize that there is nobody on earth born better than you. We all come into the world the same way, crying and naked. There will come times in your life where others are ahead of you, but you possess the ability to change whenever you want. It is one of the greatest gifts of humanity, the ability to choose to evolve. However, nothing will change unless you believe it is possible.

Next, know what you are good at and stop faulting yourself for not being the best at everything. We often times hone in on the things that somebody else can do when we can't. This is essentially us assuming that the stuff we are good at is easy for everyone because it is easy for us. Unconsciously, you are telling yourself that your talent is not a talent, and you would be a success if you just had what that other person has. However, most of the time, that person is saying the same thing. We all have a tendency to minimize ourselves; resist the temptation to do so. Recognize what you are good at, and understand that that will not include everything.

I excel at problem solving and reasoning. I am confident in saying that there is nobody I personally know who is better at looking at real world problems and creating a solution. With that being said, I am a horribly slow sprinter. I literally know dozens if not hundreds of friends and family members who can run a 40-yard dash or 100-

meter sprint faster than me. In high
school, my first girlfriend bench
pressed more than me, and it wasn't
even a substantial amount. There is
literally a laundry list of things that
other people do or have done better
than me. I am a good cook, but a lot
of my family and friends cook

> "Don't envy someone else's gift. Discover your own"
>
> Tavis Smiley

better. I am a horrible artist, a 3rd row tenor in the choir, a
below average mechanic, a sub-par farmer, a mediocre
basketball player, inept at driving a stick shift, a horrible
rancher, incompetent in heat transfer equations and the list
goes on. I want you to see this list because there was some
point in my life that one of my peers excelled in one of
these areas. But regardless of who was stronger or faster
than me, who could dunk on me, or who got a better grade
than me in school, I know that I am still a great problem
solver. Remember that other's success does not diminish
you.

Practically speaking, it is easy to say these things but
hard to do them. So here is an exercise that can help you
build confidence in your ability;

1. Come up with three positive statements about
   yourself that you absolutely know to be true. If you
   know you are Picasso reincarnated, make your
   statement "I am a great artist." If you are the strongest
   person at your school, "I am extremely strong."
2. Come up with two statements you want to be true, but
   aren't as confident about. Maybe you are a great artist
   but you are working on your business skill set, "I am
   a successful business owner." If you are a superstar
   athlete who isn't as confident about your day job "I
   am a superstar employee."

For me, I had been told most of my life that I was smart, so it didn't take me much to believe that "I am smart." I have been tutoring people since I was in the 3rd grade; so I know "I am a great tutor." Finally, whether it is a word problem or a real world scenario, I have always excelled at finding simple solutions to complex problems; so I know "I am a great problem solver." Those were my three positive statements I knew to be true.

In spite of my confidence in my intelligence, I had set some lofty goals in life. In order for me to believe that I could accomplish them, my first aspirational phrase was that "I can do anything I put my mind to." Another area where I wasn't as confident as I would like to be was in physical activities. As I previously stated, I wasn't exactly the strongest or fastest in high school. Still, I recognized that a lot of my goals took time; time that I would only have if I lived a long and healthy life. Therefore, physical fitness would be important for my long-term success, so my next aspirational phrase was simply "I am a beast." Note that these phrases are for you and you alone; so don't worry about whether other people get them or not. For me, "I am a beast" meant that I had the physical endurance, strength, and stamina to do that last rep or push through that last 100 meters. As such, I didn't have an excuse to quit.

Now that you have picked your five phrases (three confident phrases and two aspirational phrases), there is a daily exercise I want you to do. Every morning, when you wake up, and every evening before you go to bed repeat those phrases three times. Additionally, anytime when you start to doubt yourself, say all five phrases out loud or in your mind if you are in mixed company.

In addition to this verbal affirmation exercise, try what my mom fondly called "faking it 'til you make it." Within reason, in your daily life try to act in the manner you would if your aspirational statements are already true. The "within reason" part is particularly important; this is not a license to perpetrate and live outside of your means. Nor should you put yourself or anyone else in harm's way. This exercise is an opportunity for you to push yourself and deepen your resolve. If your statement is "I am a great doctor" try attending a medical seminar. If your statement is "I am the best employee at my company," try showing up an extra 15 minutes early to work.

For me, when I was working on my confidence and telling myself that "I can do anything I put my mind to," I picked up extra assignments at work. Thus, I would dedicate some time during the work week to a project that was a bit outside of my expertise or perceived skillset. This meant that sometimes I was a bioengineer working on an electrical engineering problem, or I was a lawyer working on an HR issue. As I experienced success in areas that I never believed I could excel in, it gradually made me more and more confident in saying "I can do anything I put my mind to."

Do this continuously until you believe the last two aspirational phrases as strongly as you believe the first three. When that happens, pick new aspirational phrases and repeat the process.

Establishing a strong, solid believe in yourself is a significant step towards being able to achieve. But, for me and most people, it isn't enough. No matter how confident you are in yourself there will always be something that sets you back. It could be anything from experiencing rejection from a person that you like to getting a bad evaluation or being passed over for a promotion. In situations like that, your self-confidence can be tested. A solid surface belief in yourself without a deeper belief in something greater than yourself makes you susceptible to unexpected "sinkholes" in your confidence.

Sinkholes occur when the bedrock underneath a structure is missing or erodes. This can happen for any number of reasons. When this occurs, it puts a lot of strain on the surface material. If there is anything heavy on the surface, the surface layer of the ground will buckle and a sinkhole forms destroying the surface structure.

In our analogy, your belief in yourself is the surface, and your belief in something greater than yourself is the bedrock. The bigger your goals are, the more pressure you can feel if you are relying solely on your belief in yourself to support your goals. In the context where you experience a setback, your belief in yourself can crack and crumble. If there is no greater belief supporting your self-confidence, then sinkholes can abruptly form.

Sinkholes are situations where your belief in yourself collapses under the pressure of what you are trying to accomplish. These situations can derail your progression towards your goals. However, sinkholes can be avoided by finding something greater than yourself to believe in. This will prop up your belief in yourself. By giving yourself something greater to believe in, that deeper belief acts as a bedrock to support your dreams as you strive to accomplish them. Regardless of how confident you are in yourself, your belief is going to be shaken from time to time. In those moments, it is paramount for you to believe in and be pushed by something greater than you.

The easiest example of belief in something greater than yourself that can push you is faith in God. For me, my Christianity, belief in Jesus, and faith in God are a significant reason for why I am here today. In my life, I have had numerous setbacks that could have easily halted my progress, and in some cases, came very close. In my last two years at Harvard Law School, both of my grandfathers, my great aunt who was like a grandmother to me, and my great-uncle who inspired me to attend law school all died. The belief that "…in all things God works for the good of those who love him, who have been called according to his purpose" (Rom 8:28) sustained me through trying times. So in times where I was sad or angry, or things did not go the way that I wanted them; I could fall back on the belief that somehow everything was going to work out for the best.

Furthermore, this belief in God pushed me to do more than I previously thought was possible. If I believe that "I can do all things through Christ who strengthens me" (Phil. 4:13), then that includes meeting aggressive work deadlines and acing multiple midterms in one week.

In order to accomplish great things in life, you must believe in something. Even though faith in God is a great belief to have and I would personally recommend Christianity to anyone, it is not the only belief that can push you to new heights. There are three requirements for a belief to be a basis by which you can build significant accomplishments 1. It gives you comfort in times of distress, 2. It tells you that you have potential beyond measure, and 3. You really believe in it, so don't pick something you consider far-fetched or unrealistic.

What are some examples of belief in something greater than yourself outside of religion? Family is a good example. If you come from a strong and proud family, it could be the belief that strength and excellence are hardwired into your DNA. Thus, any setback that occurs is just a temporary setback that you will easily overcome. You could believe in Karma, and that the arc of the world bends towards justice for those who are just. Or, for example, if you are a police officer or career military, you could believe in the sanctity of your brotherhood and hold true to the ideals of your organization. Other examples include your country or state constitution; the sanctity and necessity of enforcing and abiding by the laws of the land as a way to maintain equality and justice. In the words of Shepherd Book "I don't care what you believe in, just believe in it."

When you have a solid belief in yourself with a strong belief in something greater than yourself, you are ready to start building towards something exceptional.

Chapter 3:
Know What Drives You

If Belief is the ground on which your accomplishments are built, knowing what drives you is the foundation. I also like to call this "Knowing Your 'Why?'" I call it this because, knowing what drives you (e.g. your motivations) is knowing why you are willing to work harder, why you are willing to push further and why you won't quit. This is you establishing a motivation or motivations that can act as a driving force to sustain you when everything else tells you to give up.

I will not tell you it is impossible to achieve success in life without knowing what drives you and establishing solid motivations. There are numerous structures that can be built without a solid foundation. However, most structures built without a solid foundation are more temporary and fragile. So understand that if you fail to establish your foundational, core motivations you limit the heights that you can achieve. Imposing towers and magnificent monuments that stand the test of time are not built without foundations. Thus, as in the metaphor, the accomplishments you seek to build without a firm understanding of what drives you will be shorter lived.

> "... about half of what separates the successful entrepreneurs from the non-successful ones is pure perseverance"
> Steve Jobs

Put differently, nobody haphazardly breaks world records or nonchalantly achieves where so many others have failed. If you want to achieve great things, you must find the type of motivation that will push you harder than anyone else. You must find that thought that will drive you to persevere. This should be the thing that can make you jump out of bed in the morning and makes it harder to go to sleep at night.

The first thing to realize about your motivations is that they are not dependent on your course of action. A lot of the time people chose their course of action and then think of a "motivation." This is not a motivation; this is a justification for doing something you already want to do. The problem with behaving like this is it will blind you to alternative courses of action that might better serve your needs and desires.

Thus, I have found that it is more effective to identify your core motivations (e.g. establish your strong foundation) before you start working towards your goals. You need to know what drives you and use that knowledge to your advantage. Whether you love to win, help people, protect loved ones, have access, or simply hate failure, once you identify your core motivations you can use them to drive you towards extraordinary accomplishments.

H.I.P. Motivations!

H :   HONEST

I : INSPIRATIONAL

P :   PERSONAL

The second thing to realize about your motivations is that anything can be a motivation. For some people, it is as simple as wanting to be able to attract a pretty girl or handsome guy. For others, their motivations are as big as wanting to rid the world of injustice. Your motivation can be to earn a title of the best of the best, to beat somebody in a competition, or to never be hungry again. Any desire or past experience has the potential to be a motivator that drives you to achieve your goals. When you are choosing your core motivations remember the phrase "Be H.I.P." This is an acronym that captures the only three rules to abide by when choosing the core motivation to build your accomplishment on top of: 1. be Honest, 2. be Inspirational, and 3. be Personal.

Be honest with yourself! I want to lead with the biggest mistake that people make when listing motivations; they lie to themselves. Nobody else has to know what motivates you, so you gain nothing from lying other than a weak foundation to build upon. Everyone will not be motivated by pleasing God; in fact, most people won't be motivated by such an abstract target. Nor will everybody be motivated by some innate desire to help people, a love for the arts, or a love of the game. Don't lie to yourself and pretend that those are really your core motivation for success if they aren't.

I am not saying that you cannot be motivated by things outside of yourself. I had a friend in undergrad who was absolutely going to be a doctor. Yes he wanted to help people and yes he wanted to have money, but that was not the foundation for his decision to become a doctor. His primary reason for wanting to become a doctor was an unyielding desire to have the knowledge and resources necessary to take care of his parents, should they ever become ill. That motivation saw him through every all-nighter, ever cram session and every challenge, and I now have to address him as "Doctor."

There is no telling where you will find motivation. You may want to change the world or raise a family that never knows the pains of true hunger. Your motivation could be the simple desire to prove your capabilities. Whatever your motivation is, acknowledge it, accept it and be honest about it.

The reason you must be honest with yourself is that the motivation you choose will be the foundation on which you lay your goals. Goals that are not well supported by this foundation will likely fall apart. Think of the example of a promotion into management becoming available at a company. A qualified employee decides to go for the promotion because they tell themselves "I want the additional responsibility and challenge of management." The problem is that their real motivation was that they are competitive and didn't want other employees to pass them up. What will likely happen?

To answer this question you must first realize that the employee in this example did not actually want a new job, and definitely didn't want the new challenges associated with a promotion. Here, the employee really just wanted to prove they could win when competing for the promotion.

Thus, the only goal that was grounded in a core motivation was beating their coworkers out for the job. I they succeed in doing so, what happens?

The goal of being a high-quality manager is not supported by their motivation. The employee-turned-manager has already beaten out his coworkers. Unless there is another core motivation that drives them, they will have little to no real motivation to achieve the goal of being an exceptional manager. Thus, this employee will likely be subpar at their new job.

The problem does not stop there. Think about building a house. If a corner of the house fell, there is a good chance that other parts of the house will fall with it. Similarly, when a goal not supported by your true motivation falls apart, it may delay or destroy progress towards other goals. To get the promotion, the employee from our example was clearly above average at their original job. However, now this employee has become a sub-par manager. If the company decides to demote the employee back to where they began, the employee won't be worse off. But, what happens if, instead the employee is fired? That has the possibility of erasing years of working towards retirement, and the loss of income could have a strong negative impact on other goals the employee had been working towards.

Put simply, lying to yourself about your true motivations hurts you. It causes you to waste time, money and energy pursuing things that put you further from where you want to be in life. Therefore, be honest with yourself when you are identifying motivations.

Next, when choosing your core motivations, they must actually be inspiring. Whatever is your motivation for pursuing your goals must actually make you want to work harder. It has to be that thing that makes you put in an extra hour on your presentation, or proofread your work one more time.

When I was young my mom coined the phrase, "we are all motivated by crap or cravings, which one is it for you?" The premise of her question is that everybody who has done anything worthwhile has been motivated by either wanting to avoid something traumatic ('crap') or pursuing something desirable ('craving'). Most of the greatest athletes will tell you that they were pushed to greatness by a tough loss in their youth or by the desire to provide for their family. A lot of the greatest American success stories began with epic failures or lofty aspirations. There isn't a right or wrong type of motivation as long as it inspires you.

What are some concrete examples? Let's start with craving. If you are a gear head like my dad was, then you could be motivated by a car you always wanted to own. He would work hard to have extra time and money to dedicate to restoring a totaled Corvette he had acquired. That pushed him to get more done. Or maybe you are like me and have some expensive taste buds. My favorite food is crabs, especially snow crabs, and I could ramble like Benjamin Buford Blue about all the ways I like them prepared. You have not lived until you have had some well fried blue crabs or some perfectly prepared BBQ snow crabs. Growing up, whenever I brought home straight A's or won a competition my parents would make me a few clusters of crabs. That was definitely a motivator for me to do well in school growing up.

Still, I tended to be motivated best by the crap rather than the craving. A specific example of this kind of motivation is that I spent most of my life hearing people tell me what I couldn't do. No matter how many times I succeeded or defied the odds, there was always somebody there waiting to tell me I should set my sights lower. This unsolicited advice was always given with a condescending look of satisfaction. They seemed proud that they had done the good deed of saving me from the disappointment of my inevitable failure. That grated me so much! I became determined that I never wanted to see the look of satisfaction on their face from having been proved right. That motivation got me through several all-nighters and pushed me to achieve things I didn't know I could.

Ultimately, some of the greatest motivators in life will come from potentially traumatic circumstances. None of the motivators I mentioned in the previous paragraphs had as profound an impact on me as the passing of my father. There is never a good time to lose a parent, although the timing of Dad's death was especially difficult. Two months before his passing and with his support, my mom quit her job to pursue her doctorate. Thus, not only was there the hurt of that circumstance, there was also the aftermath of growing up poor, in a single parent household for the rest of my childhood. During that time, there were so many things I couldn't have that I wanted and so many experiences I never wanted to live through again. As a result, the tragedy of my dad's death fueled me more than any snow crabs or condescending teacher ever could.

Just because you endure a traumatic experience does not mean that it has to limit you or slow you down. We are all faced with tough circumstances that are outside of our control. These challenges can be things like growing up without much money, personal health challenges, instability in the household, caring for a sick family member, or even the death of a close family member. Those tragic circumstances do not define you, and they do not determine who you will be in life. You are the arbiter of your own destiny; it is within your power to determine who you will be in life. Furthermore, if you allow them, these challenges can become fuel for your passion.

> Your tragedy does not determine your trajectory!

The next thing to realize is that it is YOUR motivation! Thus, the motivation must be personal to you.

This is not about "knowing your parents why" or "knowing what your significant other thinks should drive you," nor is this chapter about the motivations of anybody but yourself. It is ok to do things for other people. There is nothing wrong with wearing a specific shirt because your girlfriend wants you to, or traveling to a new city because your husband wants you to. However, one of the biggest mistakes we make is going down a difficult path for no other reason than someone else wanting us to do so.

If my only reason for undertaking my 18-year educational goals was because my grandfather wanted one of us to be Dr. Wickliff or because I know it would have made my dad proud, I might have given up when they passed away. I know it isn't the same for everyone; for some people, the motivation to make a loved one proud grows significantly when they die. Nevertheless, what happens if you grow estranged from the person you started your journey for? Or what happens when the thought of disappointing your family just isn't as scary as it used to be? The harsh reality of relying solely on other people's desires to motivate you is that those motivations can be stolen from you at any time.

Additionally, you will never be motivated to push past your limits and excel if the source of all of your motivation is the whims and will of other people. If your motivation is not internalized, it is easy to lose sight of it. I am almost certain that your last thought going to sleep and your first thought waking up were not "I hope I make someone else proud," or "I am glad I have gotten one step closer to accomplishing another person's goal." The thing that motivates you through the hard times must be an inescapable and haunting thought. It should be a thought that, if you think about it right before bed, it can make you get out of bed to do a bit more work or set your alarm clock a few minutes earlier.

Now, this is not to say that others cannot motivate you. Even though making my dad proud is one of my motivations, it isn't the one that most drives me. If it were, I could have stopped my academic pursuits after my first degree because my dad would have already been beyond proud of me. You can have as many additional motivations as you want, but this is about finding a core motivation, which are motivations that can exist completely independent of everyone else. It is important for your core motivations to be personal because you do not want your core motivations tethered to someone or something else outside of your control.

To that end, I have a challenging, but effective exercise for those of you having difficulty finding your motivation.

1. Take a sheet of paper, and draw a line down the middle
2. Label one column "Crap"; label the other "Cravings."
3. Start with the Cravings side because it tends to be the easier column. Think of the things you most desire, but don't have or don't have enough of. If money is the first thing that comes to mind, think harder about why you want money. What are the things you most want to buy? Is it that you want to have the power to give orders instead of taking them? What are the reoccurring daydreams that always put a smile on your face? Are there things you lie in bed thinking about? It can be anything, as long as it is H.I.P. (Honest, Inspirational, and Personal). Write them down in your cravings category. "I want a new house," "I want to marry [person's name]," "I want to be my own boss," "I want this trophy," etc.
4. Now for the Crap. This is difficult; try to think of the worst experiences or feelings of your life. These would be that handful of times you felt the absolute

lowest. It could be an embarrassing experience at work, a family crisis that took a toll on you emotionally, a time when you were made fun of or any experience that you absolutely refuse to ever have again. In the Crap column, write down those feelings and experiences you never want to experience or never want to experience again. "I never want to be hungry," "I never want to bury a loved one," "I never want to let [person's name] win against me," etc.

5. Somewhere on this page are the motivations that will push you to work harder. Review the list and see which ones resonate with you the most. Ultimately your core motivation(s) will be the thing on the page that you can't stop thinking about.

6. When you find that core motivation highlight or underline those motivations.

CRAVINGS

I want to...

Own a Corvette

Beat out everyone I compete with

Have my name on a deed of land

Travel to every state in the U.S.A. and continent in the world

Eat my favorite foods whenever I want

Be called Doctor

CRAP

I NEVER want to...

Burry another loved one for a preventable reason

Fail at one of my major goals

Be unable to help my family and friends

Miss paying a bill

There are two things to note about the exercise. First and foremost, all motivations are not created equal. As I previously stated, I am far more motivated by crap than I am by cravings. The death of my dad has always been a motivating force for me. I never again want to feel the type of powerlessness and pain I felt that day. The pain of being unable to help or save someone I love. Additionally, I spent a large portion of my life with people underestimating me and writing me off. The feeling of being ignored and marginalized was something that I never again want to feel. Essentially, whether it was my 10th grade English teacher or the prelaw advisor who told me to set my law school sights lower, I became highly driven to prove people wrong when they said I couldn't or wouldn't succeed.

Secondly, know that your motivations will change over time, so update them occasionally. While I am motivated by crap more than cravings, even from a young age I loved, and still do love, gumbo and snow crabs. If I could, I would have had them all of the time; this was an example of one of my cravings. So, throughout elementary, middle school & high school, I worked hard to one day be able to afford to have gumbo & snow crabs whenever I wanted. When I went off to college I got exposed to the world of well-prepared steaks. Now, I get just as much motivation out of an excellent filet as I do a cluster or snow crabs. Thus, my cravings have changed.

At the point that you pick motivations that truly resonate with you, make sure to keep them in the forefront of your mind. My greatest motivator is working towards having the ability to take care of the people I love. Whenever I am about to go on a big interview, give a major speech, or work on a critical project; I keep reminders of that motivation around me. For me, that reminder comes in the form of something from Texas. Although I have family in major cities and small towns around the world, our family hometowns are in Liberty County – Ames, Liberty and Raywood, three adjoining towns in East Texas. For this reason, I generally wear something that reminds me of

Texas. These reminders include wearing things like my Texas flag cufflinks, cowboy belts, and memorabilia from my Texas schools. When I wear one of these items, I am reminded of all the people back home that I am working hard to protect.

If you do not have a simple portable memento that can remind you of your motivations, here is another exercise that I used when I first left for college.

1. Identify the areas you spend the most time, especially the area you spend the most time working. In college, I spent the most time at my desk and in my car.
2. Identify the items that you spend the most time with. For me those items where my three-ring binder and my laptop.
3. Place reminders of your motivations wherever you spend the most time and on whatever item or device you spend the most time with. You could place a vision board in one of these locations as well. For me, I had a board of pictures of all my family and friends on the wall in front of my desk, a cross hanging in my car on the rearview mirror, a collage of famous people I was competing with on my 3-ring binder, and a picture of a new corvette on my laptop desktop. Each of those things reminded me of something that motivated me.

Why is choosing a memento important? "The squeaky wheel gets the oil," "the nail that sticks out is most likely to get hammered," etc. There are so many sayings that essentially tell us that the thing that is the most obvious or annoying gets addressed first. It is easy to forget about an abstract concept or an old promise that motivates you. It becomes a lot harder when a constant reminder is staring you in the face on a daily basis.

Thus, the point of this exercise is to give you that constant reminder of your motivations. These mementos will keep you focused on why you do the things you do. When you embark on your journey towards making your dreams come true, you need to constantly remind yourself of why you are driven to achieve these dreams. When you lose sight of your core motivation, it can be easy to forget why you are working so hard and quit.

Quitting cannot be an option. By keeping these constant reminders around you, you make the discomfort of quitting exceed the difficulty of finishing. Understand that working towards your goals is going to get hard; worthwhile accomplishments do not come easy. For me, every time I saw a picture of a Corvette, I remembered my dad looking back at me. I thought about the people he couldn't be around to take care of and felt it was my responsibility to do so in his place. I remembered my mom, my brothers, my grandparents, and all the other people who relied on me or one day might rely on me. With those images in my head, how could I quit? How could I fail to become the man Dad expected me to be? By looking at those mementos I was reminded of my core motivations (e.g. never fail at one of my major goals, never bury another loved one for a preventable reason, etc.), and I could work harder and longer as a result.

The effect of these mementos is to make sure that you never forget these motivations. If you chose one that truly resonates with you, it can be a powerful tool in your quest to achieve your goals. An effective reminder of your core motivations will push you to do more than you might think possible and will allow you to push the limits of your capability.

Chapter 4:
Establish Goals

Goals are the framework on which accomplishment is built. Whether it is towering skyscrapers, sprawling bridges, or simple homes, every enduring structure starts off as a frame. So too should your accomplishments be framed or outlined before you start to work towards them.

How do you establish this framework? Every goal or set of goals starts as a dream. A lot of people use the words "dreams" and "goals" as if they are interchangeable, but they are not. So what is the difference between a dream and a goal? There are numerous schools of thought about this subject. I ascribe to the belief that dreams are destinations, and goals are the bricks that pave your path to a dream. Look at Dr. King's "I Have a Dream" speech. This is one of the, if not the, most well-known examples of an articulated dream. In this speech, Dr. King shares his dream for a desegregated world where equality abounds. This dream was a dream he had before he made this speech and one that was shared by many of his contemporary peers.

However, simply dreaming it was not enough. No matter how widespread or strong a dream is, a dream that is never paired with goals is never reached. To get closer to that dream of equality, Dr. King & his contemporary peers established concrete goals such as the end of Jim Crowe laws, the protection of voter's rights, the desegregation of public institutions, etc. It was the pursuit of these concrete goals that has gotten us closer to Dr. King's dream; however, all great achievements start with a dream. Thus, your extraordinary accomplishments should begin now with a dream.

> "Be strong minded and always think that the impossible is possible."
> Selena Quintanilla–Pérez

The most important thing to remember is that no dream is too outlandish, and anything is possible if you are willing to proactively work towards it. Often people do not pursue dreams because they do not believe that they have the ability to achieve them. Do not forget the groundwork of belief we established in the previous chapters. Aim as high as you can. You should believe in yourself enough to pursue any dream you can dare to dream, no matter how ambition, bold or awe-inspiring it is.

When deciding on a dream to pursue, there is no limit to what you can choose. So think about the times you fantasize about all the fantastic things you want from life. Think of all the wonderful things you lie awake imagining and daydream about. Your dream can be anything: playing in the majors, owning a business, being a surgeon, world famous artist, famous actor/actress, fighter pilot, or even a racer driver. You can dream any dream in the world, and when you find one you want to come true, the next step is to turn that dream into an emphatic statement.

I have a simple exercise for you; this is a slight variation of a leadership exercise my mom showed me.

1. Find an area where you are alone or do not mind shouting.
2. Pick a dream that you want to achieve.
3. Write it down. But, instead of writing your dream as a desire (e.g. "I want to grow my department" or "I want to be the top salesman in my region") you are going to write down your dream as if it has already occurred. Examples: "I am the newest manager at my company," "I am a successful business owner," "I am the best salesman in my region."
4. I want you to read this statement to yourself a few times.
5. Then when you are ready, state it loudly and proudly.
6. State it again, even louder.
7. Repeat step 6 five more times.

In Corporate America, they call this establishing a "vision" or "vision statement." This is essentially what your Chief Executive Officer (CEO) is doing at your annual company meeting. The CEO is loudly and clearly articulating a vision for the company. In Southern Baptist Churches, they will call this "Naming and Claiming It." The premise behind the practice is that you will never achieve a dream if you aren't able to very vocally proclaim it.

There are two reasons for this. The first is that words have power, and we often times underestimate how much they can influence our subconscious. If I tell you "Don't think about Elephants," what are you likely to have just thought about? This is why, in general, you have to be careful about what you watch and listen to. However, the power of words can be used for your benefit. If you proudly proclaim, "I am a surgeon," then you are going to vividly imagine yourself in scrubs standing in an operating room. It will be in that moment that the idea of fulfilling your dream doesn't seem as farfetched as it had in the past.

Secondly, I have found that it is easy to forget a dream, but it is much harder to forget the time you shouted "I am a successful business owner" seven times. And the louder you can proclaim your dream as a reality, the more you will believe it. If you are going to accomplish something spectacular, you cannot lose sight of or doubt your ability to reach the destination. Like Peter walking on water, the moment you start to doubt you will falter (Matt. 14:22-33). So use this exercise to fix your focus on your goals.

> "I am the greatest, I said that even before I knew I was." Muhammad Ali

Like companies who print posters of their vision statements and place them all over the office, place reminders of your proclamations around you. This can be anything from mementos that you carry to remind you of commitment to sticky notes reminders that you strategically place around your home and workspace. You should also periodically repeat the above exercise if ever you start to feel uncertain about your trajectory.

At this point, your dream is well established, you have emphatically stated it, and you have started to believe that it is possible. The next step is to turn your dream into goals. In order to do this, you must decide the 3-6 major milestones you must achieve to make your dream come true. In the case of my educational goals; my dream was to become "Dr. Wickliff." In order to accomplish that goal I knew I needed a medical degree or a Ph.D.; thus getting a Ph.D. became one of my goals. In order to get a Ph.D., you must already have two other degrees. Thus, I picked two degrees that I wanted to get prior to my Ph.D. and the three major goals that would lead me to my dream were set. My goals would be to get a B.S. in engineering, a J.D. and a Ph.D., which would allow me to make my dream of being Dr. Wickliff come true.

Consider the example of someone who dreams of becoming a professional musician, how might that translate into concrete goals? They could set a goal to learn how to read and write music. Other goals could include, scoring an album, saving the money necessary for studio time to record the album, and getting singles played on certain radio stations. With each goal they accomplish, they get closer and closer to their dream.

In establishing your goals, there are really only three rules. The first rule is that you can't achieve big dreams without big milestone goals. Using the building analogy, all structures are limited by the scope of their frame. An 80 story building has an 80 story frame. Do not expect that you will be able to achieve big dreams in life if your goals are small.

Do not expect that achieving ordinary goals will lead you to an extraordinary dream. My academic dream would not have been possible if I had not set aggressive interim academic goals. Similarly, if your dream is to be a Country Music Association Award-winning artist, your goals must be just as ambitious as that dream. Your milestone goals shouldn't be just to make an album or play a concert. Your major milestones should be the kind of goals that directly lead to your dream. Recording an album and playing at a concert are not ambitious enough goals to lead to the dream of winning a CMA Award. If that were your dream, your goals should include ambitious achievements like making a platinum selling album or going on tour with one of the previous "Entertainer of the Year" award winners. Remember, ambitious accomplishments are necessary to achieve ambitious dreams.

The second rule is that your goals must be grounded in your motivation. Think about any sturdy structure you have seen. Whenever you see a large skyscraper being built, the metal beams that comprise its framework are actually embedded into the concrete of its foundation. So too should your goals be grounded deeply in your strongest motivations. You must be able to clearly articulate why you are pursuing a goal and why that goal is meaningful to you. If you cannot, then your goals can be easily torn down.

When you are working towards exceptional achievements, you are going to want to give up at some point. I cannot tell you how many times I contemplated quitting. The ultimate determinant of your long-term success will be whether you are on a path where the pain of failure exceeds the discomfort of continued effort. If you are pursuing a goal that you don't have a strong reason for wanting, you will give up when things become difficult. The best way to combat this phenomenon is to make sure that you are highly motivated to achieve each of your goals.

So make sure that any goal you set is well grounded in a strong motivation.

The last rule is that for every one dream there should be multiple goals. In other words, you must break your dream up into digestible goals. We are going to talk later about celebrating your victories on the way to your great accomplishments; however, in order to do this, you must have smaller victories to celebrate. This step is especially crucial if you have a dream that will take years or decades to accomplish.

In general, if you fail to establish intermediate goals between you and your dream, accomplishing your dream can begin to feel overwhelming and daunting. Take, for example, my dream was to become Dr. Wickliff. My dream was not just to become Cortlan the engineer, or even Attorney Wickliff. However, by giving myself major milestones, it allowed me to feel like I was making progress. I spent eleven years in college. Without those intermediary milestones, there would have been no way for me to gauge my success or benchmark my progress. It would have been difficult to maintain my motivation to finish the last year of my journey if I hadn't accomplished anything tangible for the first ten years. For this reason, I encourage you to think carefully about how you can divide your dream into multiple goals.

Other than these three rules, you have the latitude to set whatever goals you think you can build upon to achieve your dream.

Once, you have selected your 3-6 major goals, you must refine them to make sure they are well-defined goals. An exercise that helps with this process is called setting S.M.A.R.T. Goals. You may have seen some variation of this exercise before. The premise is that ever goal you set should be a S.M.A.R.T. Goal. The acronym stands for a goal that is Specific, Measurable, Attainable, Relevant, and

Timely. So for each goal you set or think about setting for yourself try this exercise.

1. Take a sheet of paper and divide it into 5 rows.
2. In the first row write the word "Specific", in the second the word "Measurable", in the third the word "Attainable", in the fourth the word "Relevant", and in the last row write the word "Timely".

SPECIFIC	I will lose 30 pounds
MEASURABLE	I will measure success at the end by whether or not I weigh 30lbs less than when I started.
ATTAINABLE	YES!
RELEVANT	Reduces my risk of distracting health problems and gives me more energy to dedicate to working towards my goals
TIMELY	I will give myself ninety days to achieve this goal.

3. In the first row (i.e. Specific), write out your goal with specificity. This means that you shouldn't write ambiguous or imprecise statements. For example, "Getting healthier" or "Exercising more" is not a specific goal. There isn't a clear way to determine the steps you need to take to achieve any of these goals.

If you want to get healthier, a specific goal could be "Lower my blood pressure to less than 120/80. Or instead of "Exercising More," a specific goal could be to lose 30 lbs. and drop X# of pants/dress sizes. In both of those cases, I have a clear goal so that I can understand what I need to work towards. This allows me to create a concrete plan for achieving the goal. When I was first going through this exercise, I listed the specific goal of graduating with an engineering degree, a law degree, and a Ph.D.

4. In the second (i.e. Measurable) row explain how you are going to measure success. This means that generic phrases like "get better at," "do more of" or "improve" should not appear in your goal statement. When listing the specific goal of losing 30lbs and dropping a specific number of pants/dress sizes, there are clear methods I can use to determine progress towards success and when success is achieved. In the case of my academic goal, it would be in the form of 3 diplomas; I knew I had succeeded when I had received a diploma for each degree.

5. Skip the third row for now. For the fourth row (i.e. Relevant), ask yourself "is this goal relevant," and, if so, write out how this goal is relevant. What does this mean? We have talked extensively about making sure that your goals are grounded in your motivations; well this question is asking you how this goal is going to help you satisfy one or more of your motivations. The purpose of this step is to make sure that you are not going to work haphazardly towards goals. This step reminds you of why you are going to work so hard to achieve this goal. If you cannot explain the relevance of your goal, then choose a different goal. For me, there were several reasons that made my academic goals relevant. First and foremost, enough people had told me that I couldn't accomplish these

goals, which only motivated me to want to prove them wrong. Additionally, I knew that my academic journey would allow me to get a great job and grant me access that I could use to take care of my friends, family, and anyone I cared about. My salary would allow me to buy all the snow crabs and steak I wanted. Make sure that every goal you pick is grounded in strong motivators, and it helps if they are grounded in multiple.

6. In the last row, give yourself a deadline for achieving these goals. This is important because, if you give yourself infinite time to do something, you are never in jeopardy of failing to accomplish your goals. If I had said graduate with a B.S., J.D., and Ph.D. without giving myself a timetable, I could have postponed starting my journey indefinitely. When setting a timetable, be aggressive. It is okay if it ends up taking a little longer than you would like. Setting an aggressive schedule will make you work more consistently and proactively towards your goals. I recommend setting a timetable for you achieving your goal that is earlier than is actually necessary. For me, I absolutely wanted to finish all three degrees before my 26th birthday, so I made my timetable such that I would finish my last degree a year prior when I was still 24 years old. The reason for this recommendation is that setbacks are inevitable, and it is helpful to give yourself a little cushion. Ultimately, my timetable took almost a year longer than expected and had it not been for my pursuit of an aggressive timetable, I would not have accomplished my goal graduating with my B.S., J.D., and Ph.D. before my 26th birthday.

7. Now return to the third row; is your goal attainable? This section is personal to you. What I mean is that you have to believe you can achieve this goal. It

doesn't matter what anybody else thinks, all that matters is that you believe it is possible. If you don't believe you can do what you have written on this paper, edit it until you do. I emphasize the personal nature of this question, because, if you pick a lofty goal, a lot of people, including family members and friends, may tell you it is not possible. I cannot count the number of times somebody explained to me why some of my goals were unrealistic or impossible. However, none of that matters as long as you can write "YES!" in this box.

If you cannot complete this exercise for a goal, then it is likely a goal that is too ill-defined and ambiguous to pursue. When a goal is not Specific, Measurable, Attainable, Relevant, or Timely, it is hard to define when success is achieved and even harder to understand your relative progress. Not knowing how close you are to success and not being able to determine how much progress you have made, can make it hard to maintain your determination. Furthermore, when you believe a goal is unattainable, you will lack motivation from the beginning. Thus pursuing goals that are not SMART Goals can be frustrating, and increases the likelihood that you quit.

Therefore, if you are unable to complete this exercise with a particular goal, refine the goal more before you attempt to develop a plan to achieve it. In some cases, this will require you to completely reevaluate your goals, and in others, it will just require a little tweaking. Regardless, do not actively pursue a goal that is not Specific, Measurable, Attainable, Relevant and Timely.

Chapter 5:
Create a Plan

When you are laying the framework for your accomplishment, you will set goals that can be measured in months or years. That is the framework that we established in the previous chapter. Yet, in order to achieve milestone goals that are long-term, you are going to have to achieve shorter-term goals along the way. The next step in your personal construction project is to create your detailed blueprint of those short-term goals. The aim of this chapter is to identify the steps necessary to achieve your milestone accomplishments and your dream.

In this chapter, you will learn methods for creating a thorough plan to achieve your dream. You may ask, "Why is this necessary, I already know what I need to do?"

Knowing where you want to end up is not the same thing as knowing exactly how to get there. Most major milestones require dozens if not hundreds of intermediary steps to achieve them. These steps include things like consent forms, submission

> "... tomorrow belongs to those who prepare for it today"
> Malcolm X

deadlines, and required signatures. If you don't take the time to identify all those intermediate steps, it is likely that you will miss some of them. Those kinds of lapses can be costly. I know people who have had their journeys delayed by over a year because they failed to turn in a one-page form in a timely manner.

Additionally, the planning process, if done properly, will allow you to identify potential stumbling blocks before you encounter them. This gives you an opportunity to plan for difficult circumstances before they occur. Thus, planning increases the likelihood that you successfully navigate through tough situations and avoid pitfalls.

The technique I recommend for creating your plan is to plan forward and backwards. What does that mean? A forward plan is where you make a list of the tasks and steps you must complete to meet your major milestone goals. So let us use the example of a road trip from downtown Austin, TX to Houston, TX. If you were planning forward, you would start from downtown Austin and plan the road and highways you need to take to get to Houston. One of the shortest and most straightforward routes is to take Interstate 35 to Hwy 290 East which dead ends in Houston. This is the likely route people, and most GPS systems, would pick to get to Houston from Austin.

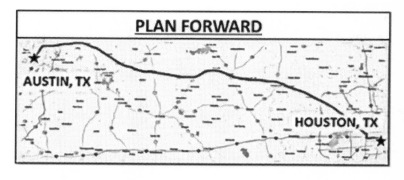

Planning backwards is when you start with the goal and plan from the goal to your starting position. Your plan starts with the step that must immediately precede the accomplishment, then the step that must precede that step, and so on until you get to your starting position. Going back to our road trip example, if you were planning backwards, you would start from Houston. The first step would be to ask which highways go in the direction of Austin. You will find that Interstate 10, as well as Highway 290, are potential routes towards Austin. Once on those two highways, there are multiple routes to get to Austin. You would trace backwards on each of those routes and see all of the different ways that they can get you to Austin. In this context, planning backwards generates more than a half dozen different routes.

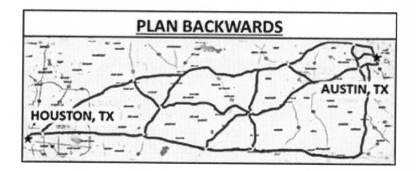

"If you fail to plan, you plan to fail!"

Individually, planning forward and planning backwards can be useful tools for creating a plan. However, depending on how you think, using one method without the other can lead to less thorough planning. The reason for planning both forward and backwards is that it forces you to consider alternate possible pathways to your goal. By approaching the problem from different vantage points, you can force yourself to think outside of the box. In the previous example, forward planning only yielded one route. Whereas, approaching the problem from the backwards perspective gave us multiple, more detailed route options. Sometimes the opposite is true, and forward planning is the method that allows you to generate multiple possible, detailed approaches. Thus using both methods simultaneously is a powerful tool to creating plans for long-term goals.

Consider the real-world example of my wanting to become Dr. Wickliff and work in a technical field. When I planned forward, I thought I had to get a bachelor's degree, and then go to medical school, and complete a residency, at which point my elementary school goal would have been accomplished. But, medical doctors are not the only people with the title doctor. So when I started from the goal and worked backwards, I realized that I could get a medical degree, a pharmaceutical doctorate, a doctorate in veterinary medicine, or get a Ph.D. in any number of disciplines including the science, technology and engineering fields. The first step in this backwards planning opened up several options that I might not otherwise know existed.

Now I want you to do a planning forward and backwards exercise. The more thoroughly you do your backwards and forward planning the more options you give yourself in accomplishing your goals and the clearer your action items become. If done properly, this exercise might cause you to change some of your major milestones that you established in the previous section. That is okay; the most important thing is that you still make sure that any goal you set, big or small, major or intermediary, is a S.M.A.R.T. Goal.

1. Start by planning forward.
2. This may end up taking more space than one sheet of paper, but for now, let's start with one sheet of paper.
3. Write on the top-left corner "now".
4. On the bottom-right corner write whatever your big dream is.
5. In between the two points, I want you to write the 3-6 major milestones that made up your framework from the previous chapter. Do your best to space them out evenly.
6. In between now and the first milestone write out 3 major steps that must occur before you can reach the first milestone. Do your best to space them out evenly.
7. Repeat step 6 between each of the major milestones until you get to the final accomplished dream. If you have already identified multiple possible pathways to your dream, write them down as well. If you run out of space, do this on another sheet of paper.
8. Now plan backwards. This tends to be the less linear because you find pathways you didn't know existed.

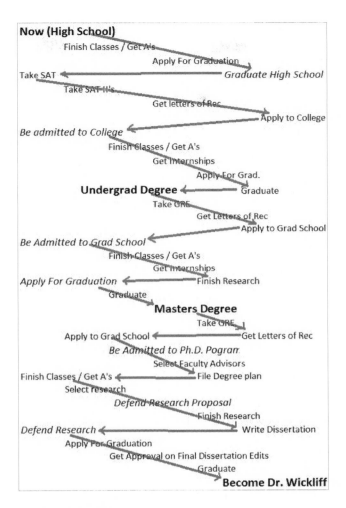

9. Get another sheet of paper.
10. Write on the top-left corner "now".
11. On the bottom-right corner write whatever your big dream is.

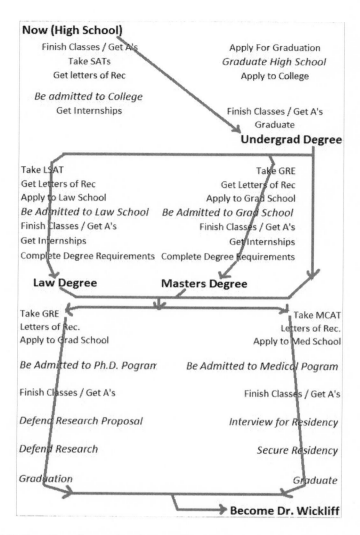

Now (High School)
Finish Classes / Get A's
Take SATs
Get letters of Rec

Be admitted to College
Get Internships

Apply For Graduation
Graduate High School
Apply to College

Finish Classes / Get A's
Graduate
Undergrad Degree

Take LSAT
Get Letters of Rec
Apply to Law School
Be Admitted to Law School
Finish Classes / Get A's
Get Internships
Complete Degree Requirements

Take GRE
Get Letters of Rec
Apply to Grad School
Be Admitted to Grad School
Finish Classes / Get A's
Get Internships
Complete Degree Requirements

Law Degree   **Masters Degree**

Take GRE
Letters of Rec.
Apply to Grad School

Be Admitted to Ph.D. Pogram

Finish Classes / Get A's

Defend Research Proposal

Defend Research

Graduation

Take MCAT
Letters of Rec.
Apply to Med School

Be Admitted to Medical Pogram

Finish Classes / Get A's

Interview for Residency

Secure Residency

Graduate

Become Dr. Wickliff

12. Starting from the dream list the steps that precede or could precede the accomplishment of your dream.
13. Then List the steps that precede or could precede the steps listed.
14. Repeat this process until you work your way back up to "now".

15. Anytime one of your pathways leads back to one of your previously selected major milestones circle them.

16. Compare the backwards and forward planning: Were there any pathways that did not include your previously selected milestones? Consider whether there are other major milestones you should pursue. Typically, the first time you do forward and backwards planning for a goal, the papers do not look the same. If they are identical in the first iteration, perform research to see if you are missing any steps or possible alternative pathways.

17. Were there major steps or other goals that were included on multiple pathways? If you have multiple possible pathways you can choose to get to the same destination, identifying steps that are on multiple pathways can afford you more options as you progress through your journey. An example of this could be an accountant with the dream of starting a business. The accountant is uncertain whether they want to start a general store, a delivery company or a property management company. As one of the prerequisites to starting a company, this accountant needs work experience. To get this work experience, the accountant can choose to either work at a property management company or work at a venture capital firm. Which job should the accountant take? If the accountant works for a property management company as an accountant, the experience may not be transferrable to other businesses. Yet, if the accountant works with a venture capital firm, the experience raising money will be transferable to any business. Thus the accountant should strongly consider working at the more generally applicable position (i.e. the venture capital firm). Choose

pathways that allow you the most opportunities to achieve your dreams.

18. What are the steps that both the forward and backwards plans have in common? These steps will likely be non-optional steps.

19. Throughout this process, you will gather more information about steps and pathways you didn't know existed. Consider repeating this process once or twice to refine your forward and backwards plan.

20. Based on the final backwards and forward pathways, select a combined plan which includes "now," 3-6 major milestones, your dream and at least 3-5 intermediate steps between each one of them. This is your blueprint.

Doing this process in an electronic spreadsheet or in some other form of computer program may prove easier. Especially if your goals could be intricate or you are still figuring out what steps each goal entails. This also allows you to easily edit and expand your goals and the intermediate steps.

> "A person has to remember that the road to success is always under construction... it is not easy becoming successful"
> Steve Harvey

Even when you finish this process, you are not finished with your plan. This plan that you have generated in this chapter is only a starting point. Your plan is a "living document." That means that, like all living things, it should consume, grow and adapt.

What does a plan consume? Information! As you progress through your journey you are going to learn more about the steps to achieving your goals. The first day I began each of my degrees, I was given a degree plan and/or graduation requirements. These were checklists that contained every step I needed to complete in order to graduate. Similarly, whenever I would start a new job or new project at work, I would be given expectations and project goals. Whether formally written or given in an informal conversation, this information provided me an understanding of what I needed to be successful on the job. Whether you get the information as part of a formal document, find it while looking online or get it from a conversation with a trusted resource, whenever you gain more information on how to accomplish a major or intermediary step it should be incorporated into your plan.

The incorporation of new information into your plan means that it is going to get bigger. Your plan should grow over time. This doesn't have to all be captured on one sheet of paper, or in one excel file. As you expand your plan you will likely engage in forward and backwards planning for several of your intermediate steps and milestone goals. Thus you will have several checklists, flowcharts, and diagrams that constitute your total plan. This is a good thing! Just make sure to never lose sight of your overall dream while pursuing a major goal, and don't lose sight of your milestone goals while completing intermediate steps.

The last way in which your plan will resemble a living organism is that it should adapt to changing circumstances. As will be discussed in later chapters, there will be unforeseen circumstances that make your plan infeasible, impractical, or inefficient. In those circumstances, failing to change your plan could result in you failing to accomplish your dream. Do not be so fixated on adhering to the plan, that you miss opportunities to achieve your goals and dreams. You cannot be expected to account for everything that might happen a year from now, let alone five or ten years from now. As you get new information and circumstances change, adapt!

Chapter 6:
Start Building!

A completed work is far more impressive than a planned masterpiece. Often times we let the quest for "great" be the enemy of achieving "good" and get stuck in a pattern of analysis paralysis. Analysis paralysis occurs when you over-analyze a decision or action to the point that you never actually make a choice and end up in a paralyzed or inactive state. Essentially, we often continue to outline, and plan, and revise, and amend, and basically, do everything BUT act.

There are three main reasons that we end up in a state of analysis paralysis: 1. Chasing the Perfect Plan; 2. Fear of Failure; and 3. Fear of Success.

Let's start by dispelling the myth of the perfect plan. Sometimes we get caught in a state of analysis paralysis because we believe that we can create a perfect plan that ensures failure is impossible. Planning is a great thing, and

> "If you spend too much time thinking about a thing, you'll never get it done"
> Bruce Lee

all the best accomplishments begin with a plan. Still, you must realize that in life there is no such thing as a perfect plan, and the only result of pursuing a perfect plan is a failed accomplishment.

The only sure way to fail at something is to never try. And if you are spending your energy trying to create a "perfect plan" that accounts for every detail, you are almost certain to never actually start. There will always be a new detail to account for or something that you can't know at the onset of a major undertaking. Therefore, if you make beginning your journey contingent on knowing exactly what the outcome will be, you will forever be stuck in the planning phase. Therefore, you will never actually accomplish anything.

Put differently, how would you feel if your builder told you that they couldn't start the build until you finalized the carpet in your house? Would it make sense not to start the building process until the color of the kids' rooms' walls were chosen and finalized? This premise is laughable. Homeowners know that any number of things can affect the "final touches" like paint and flooring over the course of a lengthy build. The lighting in the house could make certain colors look different, the originally selected fixtures can become unavailable at the time of installation, or you could just suddenly realize that the flooring you thought was pretty, now disgusts you. Anybody who has ever gone through the home building process can tell you that there is really no predicting how things might change, but progress must continue. In the end, the exterior paint does not affect the wall construction, and the showerhead does not affect the house plumbing.

So if the premise of delaying construction of your dream home until you pick the countertops is ridiculous, why is it that we often times will delay undertaking our dreams until we know exactly how every minor detail is going to work out?

You tell yourself that I can't apply to college until I know exactly what career I want. Or I can't apply for an opportunity until I am absolutely sure that I will get it or that once I get it I will accept the opportunity. Or I can't go on a date with someone until I am absolutely certain that I will marry them. When planning our lives, we often avoid starting the beginning of a process until we feel that we know exactly where it is going to end. We try to analyze and plan every little detail before we start the journey, which is like refusing to start a long road trip unless you know every gas station that you are going to stop at along the way. However, there is no possible way for you to know every pit stop and detour that a thousand mile journey will have.

Similarly planning out every detail of your life before you live it is impossible. There is no way to know exactly what tomorrow will hold. Just like you expect that your builder will start constructing the walls of your house even before you know what you want to paint them, you should expect that you will start working towards your goals even before you know exactly where they will end.

Thus, dispel the notion that a plan can be perfect, or that a plan can account for every eventuality. If you have established a strong framework,

> A completed work is far more impressive than a planned masterpiece.

be comfortable with a bit of ambiguity and start building your future.

The other reason that people often get caught in a state of analysis paralysis is to avoid facing their fear. There are two fears that most paralyze us. The first is the fear of failure and the second is the fear of success.

Fear of failure is something that can often cause analysis paralysis. We are so afraid that we may fail that we never try. What is worse is that this kind of analysis paralysis often times results in you eventually just abandoning the pursuit. A perfect example of this is walking up and talking to somebody. Think about the time there was that person you really wanted to talk to, but you were afraid to get shot down. You stared and planned and thought and analyzed, but you never actually walked up and initiated a conversation. Eventually, that person leaves the room, and you tell yourself that you were better off for not having tried.

> "Throw caution to the wind and just do it."
> Carrie Underwood

I am certain that if you take inventory over your life, you will see that there were so many times that your fear of failure caused you to never try. Whether it was the job you didn't apply for because you didn't think you could get it, or the college you didn't apply to because you thought you didn't have a chance at admissions. Maybe it was the mentor you never developed a relationship with because you were afraid to approach them or the raise you never got because you didn't want to ask. At some point or another, in our lives, we have passed up an opportunity because we were so afraid of failure we didn't try.

When trying to get past the fear of failure, there are three things I remind myself.

1. The only sure way to fail at something is to never try. Thus, being overtaken by a fear of failure is the only sure way that you will fail to accomplish something.

2. The word "No" never hurt anybody. Most of the time, the failure that we are so afraid of is hearing somebody tell use "no." Often times, we inflate how harmful hearing the word "no," is, and create these elaborate scenarios to convince ourselves it will be a great trauma. Nevertheless, at the end of the day, it is just a word. Most of us learned in elementary school "sticks and stones may break my bones but words will never hurt me." If you remember that lesson you will find it laughable to not try for fear of a rejection. When looking for an opportunity, you may have to apply dozens if not hundreds of times to get a handful of interviews and eventually one success. Nevertheless, that is a small price to pay for that success, and once you have it, the dozens of no's won't matter.

In cases where there is a greater consequence than a simple "no," you may be experiencing "apprehension of failure." The apprehension of failure is something different that we will address later in the chapter. Still, if the only consequence of failure is hearing the word "no," go for it! Remember that nobody will remember those kinds of failures; they will only remember your success. If you think of the most famously successful people in the world, they have failed far more times than they have succeeded. Nobody cares about the hundreds, if not thousands of times Edison failed when making the lightbulb. Nobody remembers the hundreds of shots your favorite basketball player missed in practice. Likewise, nobody is going to care about or remember the rejection letters you got on

> "Faith is taking the first step even when you don't see the whole staircase"
> Dr. Martin Luther King, Jr.

your way to your Dream College, career, or business.

3. If in the moment, I am still being paralyzed with fear, I ask myself a question. "On my deathbed will it haunt me more if I try and fail or never try at all?" Unless I can honestly say "I would regret it more to try and fail," then I will force myself to go for it.

Fear of failure is a concept that most of us are familiar with, but I would imagine that "fear of success," sounds a bit... crazy. Who would be afraid of being successful? Although fear of success seems like an odd concept, it is a fear that most people have experienced. You remember being in class and knowing the answer to the question, but being too nervous to raise your hand? Or how about that time your boss asked for people to work on a new project, and even though you really wanted to volunteer because it sounded like a perfect fit, you sat quietly in the back of the room? Why were you afraid? What is at the root of this fear?

The first answer that comes to mind is "I was afraid I was wrong", or that "I was afraid I would fail." As we previously discussed, sometimes that is a very real fear, but that wasn't why you didn't volunteer. You were certain that you knew the answer to that question, and you knew you were the best person for that job. So why didn't you volunteer? Marianne Williamson said it best:

"Our deepest fear is not that we are inadequate. Our deepest fear is that we are powerful beyond measure. It is our light, not our darkness that most frightens us. We ask ourselves, 'Who am I to be brilliant, gorgeous, talented, fabulous?' Actually, who are you not to be? You are a child of God. Your playing small does not serve the world. There is nothing enlightened about shrinking so that other people won't feel insecure around you. We are all meant to shine, as children do. We were born to make manifest the glory of God that is within us. It's not just in some of us; it's in everyone. And as we let our own light shine, we

unconsciously give other people permission to do the same. As we are liberated from our own fear, our presence automatically liberates others."

Put less eloquently, one of our biggest fears is standing out and being different. When you are successful, you stand out. The person who is successfully moving up the ranks will get more and more responsibility at work. As a result, they will work longer hours and have less time to hang out with their old friends. If you are working hard to make it to the next level as an athlete, you aren't going to be able to join in with everyone else drinking and eating whatever they want. And the list goes on, whether it is sounding different because you are studying vocabulary to do well in school, or prioritizing new things because you are trying to reach a new level, anytime you strive for new success it is going to make you seem different to the crowd you used to hang out with. And that fact is scary.

The reason being different is scary, is because it can go hand and hand with the fear of isolation. You start asking yourself questions like:

"What happens if my old friends don't get what I am trying to do?"

"What happens if I don't make new friends where I am trying to go?"

"What if I am not accepted anymore?"

"What if I am not cool anymore?"

"Will they look at me funny?" etc.

I was blessed; most of my differences are very evident and hard to hide. So I have been considered different, weird, and/or strange my whole life. Throughout the majority of my scholastic career, I was the only or one of the only black kids in my class. Then I had the audacity to think it was acceptable to skip grades, so I spent the majority of my scholastic career 1-4 years younger than everyone in my classes. Furthermore, I chose engineering and legal professions; so once I entered the world of work,

I was always the youngest and typically one of the only black men in my areas of the company. Thus, most of my life, I embraced being different because I had no other choice. When people would ask me how it feels being different because of my age, my ethnicity, my occupations, my education, etc. I coined a phrase "I am the only me I have ever been, so it feels normal to me."

Why would I call that a blessing? Well, I assure you that sticking out like a sore thumb regardless of my environment was not always something I viewed as a blessing. I have pretty much been getting picked on since the day I was born. I walked into most situations knowing I would not quite fit in. So rather than focusing on trying to fit in, I just committed to unapologetically being the best me I could be. Thus, the blessing was that for most of my life I never had to make the choice to be different or stand out, it was made for me.

I say most of my life, because there were definitely times when I found cliques of people that I could assimilate into. In those moments where I had to decide between going with a comfortable flow and being true to my ambition, I was forced to make some of the most difficult choices of my life. The time that most illustrates why those types of decisions are difficult was my choice to complete my Ph.D.

When you graduate from a top tier law school, it is expected that you will either work for a major law firm or take a prestigious public interest or government job. This is what the vast majority of my classmates did coming out of Harvard Law School, but I went to law school knowing that I had no intention of doing either. As I said earlier, I knew I was going to go straight from law school to a Ph.D. program. Yet, after three years of belonging to a group of people, the idea of breaking away from that group was scary. And it felt like there were only so many times I could ignore so many people telling me how unnecessary a

Ph.D. would be. Did I really want to break away from the crowd and do something different?

There were numerous times where the answer to that questions was "no." I sincerely tried to go with the flow and get a job at a great law firm. However, the closer I got to graduation the more uncomfortable I felt. Because my goals were well grounded in my core motivations, the idea of abandoning was not an option. Yet, I was still afraid to take the next step, but why?

As I said, this wasn't a fear of failure. There was never a moment where I imagined failing my Ph.D. program. If not a fear of failure, what was it? It was the fear of being isolated from the people I had grown so close to. I would be on a different trajectory than my friends, which meant I would have less time to see them. Also, what if they think I am ridiculous for pursuing an 'unnecessary degree'?

Ultimately, there were three things that I told myself to get through. 1. Discomfort is a part of growth 2. It is harder work trying to fit in and 3. Everything isn't for everyone.

One of the most physically exhausting two weeks of my life occurred very recently. After finishing my last degree, I decided that I was going to take some time off, write and get a bit more in shape. I shared these plans with my friend, a former professional track athlete turned trainer named Andrea Jackson, and she invited me to train with her in Bermuda. For some reason, I thought that doing two-a-days with a former heptathlete was a great way to celebrate my graduation, so I packed my bags.

The first day I trained with her, I threw up and passed out, and then came back that afternoon to train again. What made the training program so effective was that it constantly got more challenging. One of her favorite things to tell her clients is "get uncomfortable." If you can get through a set of one of her circuit workouts and you don't feel discomfort, do more until you do. If ever a circuit got too easy, she would create a new one. The rationale is that discomfort is the beginning of growth. If you are stretching your capabilities and reaching for something that you have never achieved before, you will feel discomfort along the way.

How does this story relate to you achieving your goals? For those two weeks, I felt like I was going to break and existed in a constant state of discomfort. Nevertheless, at the end of those two weeks, I had made more progress towards my fitness goals than I had in the last two months. What I learned in that experience, and you can learn from that story, was that you can't become your best while staying in your comfort zone. That is a principle that doesn't just apply to working out.

I understand that crowds are comfortable and standing up on your own can be quite uncomfortable. However, in order to remain a part of the crowd, you are going to have to constantly diminish yourself so that you don't stand out. Thus, it is impossible for you to maximize who you are if you are content staying in the comfort zone of the crowd.

Yes, leaving the comfort zone of the crowd feels awkward and uncomfortable. Coming out of law school, it was incredibly uncomfortable to leave guaranteed employment behind to pursue my passion. But remember that discomfort is the beginning of all growth. Had I stayed on the comfortable path, I would have only gained legal experience. By leaving my comfort zone, I was able to grow as an engineer and businessmen while still growing as a lawyer. The discomfort you feel when you make yourself stand out and step up to a new level of responsibility or try to achieve a new level of success is a natural part of the process. Thus if I am not a little uncomfortable, I am probably not doing my best.

I find that it is always harder to fight against your true ambition. There is a concept called cognitive dissonance;

this is a form of mental stress that you experience when your actions are inconsistent with your beliefs. In other words, it is more difficult to do something that you don't want to do than it is to do something you believe in. This is the scientific basis for the old adage, "If you are doing something you love, you never work a day in your life." The principle is that if you believe in and love your work, you find it easier to do.

I have worked jobs where I struggled to get through a basic 8-hour workday. I felt so tired and questioned whether I could make it through the work week. While I was pursuing my doctorate degree, I was a fulltime student taking the maximum allowed credit hours every semester. Additionally, I worked 30-40 hours per week as legal counsel for a pharmaceutical company, while working 10-20 hours a week as a teaching assistant/lecturer. I did all of this while traveling around the country speaking. There were literally weeks where I worked over 80 hours. Nevertheless, I felt more energetic and happy after a 14-hour day of doing things that I was passionate about than I did after an 8-hour day of doing what I disliked.

I am sure you have experienced this phenomenon in your personal and professional life. That is not just your imagination! Your brain works harder when you do something you hate or act against your desires. Thus, it is literally harder for you to do work that doesn't help you achieve a goal. So the question I asked myself, and the question I am asking you is, "Why

> "Follow your passion. Stay true to yourself. Never follow someone else's path unless you're in the woods and you're lost and you see a path. By all means, you should follow that."
> Ellen DeGeneres

work more to do something you want less?"

Ultimately, the realization that resonated with me the most was that not everything is for everyone. We have all heard that phrase before. Yet, something that we overlook about that phrase is that, implied in it is, "everything is for someone." The most eye-opening experience for me was having the pleasure of meeting people who were born to stand in a courtroom. Ultimately meeting some real litigators in training was what made me certain I needed to be on a different path. There is nothing like listening to somebody who has found their purpose in life talk about their job. Everything about the courtroom fascinated them, and they could joyfully ramble about everything from meeting a client to using an obscure rule of evidence. That is the kind of joy you only experience when you are pursuing your dreams, and I realized that I wanted that type of joy.

When you are pursuing your passion, you are not necessarily going to love everything you do. All of us have to make some sacrifices to achieve our dreams. However, when you are pursuing something you truly believe in and desire, even the mundane and annoying aspects of your job are easier. Seeing people with that type of contentment with their work strengthened my resolve. The crowd I was in found their passion, and it just happened to be different than mine. Once I made that realization, I decided that needed to pursue something I could be that passionate about.

When you began reading this book, there was a dream that you weren't sure if you should dare to dream. By now you have crystalized that dream into some very concrete goals. Now you may be like I was going into my last year of law school, letting fear deter you

> "You can't make decisions based on fear and the possibility of what might happen"
> Michelle Obama

from taking that next big step. I took that leap into the unknown, and three years later I couldn't imagine having made a different decision. There is nothing I could have achieved in the courtroom that compares to the joy I felt when my committee chair, Dr. César Malavé, shook my hand and called me doctor. Ultimately, joy is worth the risk.

Despite all of what I have said in the chapter, I understand being leery of starting to build towards your dreams. I know sometimes taking the first steps in a journey can be extremely intimidating, especially if you have set some lofty goals. Coping with the fear of beginning a new chapter in your life or undertaking a new goal is not easy, but it is something you can accomplish.

The first step in coping with and overcoming your analysis paralysis is to differentiate between helpful apprehension and debilitating fear. Your apprehension can be healthy, but fear is not. The problem is that they are sometimes hard to distinguish between. Both apprehension and fear result in you feeling an uneasy aversion to proceeding with an action. I am sure you have a clear understanding of debilitating fear, but what is helpful apprehension?

We have already talked about how everything that makes you uncomfortable is not necessarily bad. Helpful apprehension is one of those useful uneasy feelings. Healthy apprehension is your mind making you aware of a present danger that you may otherwise be ignoring, which is helpful. In moments where you are going to make a risky investment or take a leap of faith in your career, you should have at least considered the aspects of that risk that make you uneasy.

The exercise I use to help me differentiate between debilitating fear and helpful apprehension is to list out the pros and cons. However, the exercise I use is a modified

version of risk assessment used in project management.
The exercise is as follows:

1. Draw a vertical line down the middle of the page.
    Title the first column "Pros" and the second column
    "Cons".
2. In your pros column list out all of the possible
    benefits to making this decision.
3. In your cons column list out all of the possible
    downsides to making this decision.
4. Now turn the sheet over. This time, draw a line down
    the middle vertically and across the middle
    horizontally. What you should have is four rectangles
    drawn on your paper or a 2 x 2 grid.
5. Label the first column "Pros" and the second column
    "Cons".
6. In the top row of your Pros column, I want you to list
    out all the certain or near certain positive outcomes
    from the decision you are making. In this context
    "near-certain" can be anything that you consider more
    than 90% likely to occur.
7. In the top row of the Cons column, list every certain
    or near-certain negative outcome of a decision. In this
    context "near-certain" can be anything that you
    consider more than 75% likely to occur. The reason
    this is a lower standard is so you can more easily
    identify risks to be mitigated.
8. In the bottom row of the Pros column, write out the
    best possible scenario you could reasonably expect. I
    emphasize reasonable expectations because this
    should not be the absolute most extreme circumstance
    that you could imagine. For example, it is not a
    reasonable expectation that going on a school field
    trip could result in you getting bit by a radioactive
    spider and becoming a real life Spiderman.

9. Similarly, in the bottom row of the Cons column, write out the worst possible scenario you could <u>reasonably</u> expect.
10. Now ask yourself the following questions:
    a. Does the worst possible scenario of my actions result in my or anyone else's serious injury, significant financial loss, incarceration, or death?
    b. Do the cons I wrote in either of the front or back sections outweigh the pros?
    c. Is the result essentially outside of my control, and I have no ability to diminish the likelihood of any of these negative outcomes listed?

If the answer to any of these questions is "yes," then you are probably experiencing some helpful apprehension that should be addressed. But, if the answer to all of these questions is "no," then what you are probably experiencing is debilitating fear. In which case, you should ignore your unease and move forward. Later in this chapter, we will talk about some techniques for overcoming fear.

"But we also believe in taking risks, because that's how you move things along" Melinda Gates

You will never make a worthwhile decision that does not have some inherent risk. The adage, "no risk, no reward," is a true statement. The point of this exercise is to make sure that the potential reward outweighs the risk. You can also use this exercise to identify places where risk can be limited or mitigated.

As an example of this exercise, let's say that you are thinking about going skydiving. Although you think it is going to be fun, you are feeling uneasy about going through with it. Is this uneasiness helpful apprehension or debilitating fear? I completed the previous exercise for going skydiving. Generally, most people who go skydiving feel that the pros outweigh the cons. They get a great conversation starter, have some exciting videos, and after they get over the initial fear of jumping out of a plane, they find the experience quite fun. Additionally, there is a lot you can do to control how positive your outcomes are for your skydive. You can go through proper training, verify the safety of your parachute, jump while being harnessed to an experienced jumper, and the list goes on. However, the worst possible outcome of skydiving is death or serious bodily harm.

GOING SKYDIVING (front)	
PROS	CONS
Good Conversation Starter	Cost money
Fun experience	Possibly dangerous
Bonding opportunity for me and whoever I go with	Likely going to be frightening
Sense of fulfillment by checking something off of my bucket list	

GOING SKYDIVING (back)	
PROS	CONS
I will have a get to "fly" really fast.	I will be terrified jumping out of the plane, and might have a couple of embarrassing moments as a result
I will have a cool video and story to share.	
The experience of skydiving is incredibly enjoyable and I have a cool story to tell.	I die because something goes wrong and my parachute does not function properly.

Thus, you can answer "no" to the second two questions, but the answer to the first questions is "yes." Therefore, the unease you feel about skydiving is helpful apprehension. This does not mean that you shouldn't skydive. It means that you should take as many precautions as you can to ensure that you have a positive experience (e.g. train, check reviews on the company, safety checks, etc.). Some of your unease should subside when you take those reasonable precautionary steps.

Now consider the example of asking someone to be your mentor. You are in a room and you see somebody who is in the field you want to work in and doing the kind of work that you want to do. There is nobody around them. This is a great opportunity to walk up to them and spark a conversation. Yet, you have an uneasy feeling that is keeping you frozen. Is this unease helpful apprehension or debilitating fear?

ASKING SOMEONE TO BE YOUR MENTOR (front)	
PROS	CONS
Possibility that I learn a lot	Feels a little awkward starting a conversation with someone
Likely to get a good conversation	They could say "no"
May get a lifelong mentor	
Exposure to possible job opportunities	
Future Guidance	

ASKING SOMEONE TO BE YOUR MENTOR (back)	
PROS	CONS
I will at the very least get some advice and have a brief conversation	I will feel awkward starting a conversation with this person
I get a lifelong mentor and friend who can give me access to life changing opportunities	I get told "no," and have to endure some awkwardness as a result

Using the same exercise; we see that there is no real downside to attempting to start a conversation with this person. The only cons to approaching them are that they may tell you "no," and you may feel embarrassed. Conversely, you are likely to have a good conversation and get valuable information that will help you get closer to your goals. As such, the potential pros far outweigh the cons in every regard.

Additionally, the worst possible scenario does not result in any real harm. The worst possible scenario is a bit of rejection and an awkward exchange. As I have previously stated, the word "no" is nothing to be afraid of and causes no real harm.

You have an exceptional amount of control over whether or not you have a good conversation with this person and gain a mentor out of this interaction. If you can make a connection with this person and sell them on why you would make a great mentee, you will likely get the positive outcome you are seeking.

This means that the answer to all three of the follow-up questions to this exercise (i.e. 1. Somebody gets hurt? 2. Cons outweigh pros? 3. Outcome outside your control?) are "no." Thus, what you are experiencing is debilitating fear you should ignore.

The idea of fear being debilitating is pretty commonplace, but saying "helpful apprehension," may seem odd. Why is apprehension helpful? First and foremost it can help you avoid pitfalls. We talked earlier about there being multiple routes you can take to get to your dreams. Not all routes are created equal. If you dream about owning a multimillion dollar business, there are immoral, illicit, and illegal manners for achieving that dream. Thus, if you feel uneasy before starting down the very difficult and dangerous path of trying to become the next Pablo Escobar, then that is not fear. That uneasy feeling is helpful apprehension suggesting that you choose a different path.

Helpful apprehension can not only prevent you from starting down the wrong path, but it can also keep you on the correct path. We talked earlier about fear of failure, causing analysis paralysis. Now let us talk about the apprehension of failure. Whereas fear will paralyze, apprehension will make you proceed cautiously and purposefully towards a destination.

When pursuing your dreams, the negative consequences of failing or giving up outweigh the benefits of quitting. Thus, you should have an apprehension of failing at achieving your dreams. This apprehension of failure has been something that has stuck with me my entire life. I have always pushed myself. Whether it was telling everyone I knew that I was going to get a Ph.D. before I turned 26, taking over all the legal work for a company of a couple hundred employees the day after passing the bar exam, or even the deadline I gave myself to write this book, I often feel like I bite off

> "The future rewards those who press on. I don't have time to feel sorry for myself. I don't have time to complain. I'm going to press on"
> Pres. Barack Obama

more than I can chew. In those moments, my apprehension of failing (i.e. the uneasy feeling of letting people down, going back on my word, failing to deliver, etc.) pushes me to keep working towards my goal no matter how much I want to stop. As a result of the desire to avoid failure, I press forward until I achieve success.

Perhaps one of the best examples of this phenomenon was when I started college. I was admitted into college as a 14-year-old high school sophomore, and I started college a week after my 15th birthday. The night before classes started, I can picture my fresh 15-year-old-self sitting in my dorm thinking "what the heck did I just do?" I gave up 2 years of additional preparation for college curriculum, to live on my own while taking a ridiculous first-year curriculum. What made this feeling worse was when I sat in my room and calculated that I could have graduated undergrad in about the same time had I stayed in high school. Between having an additionally two years of AP credit and dual enrollment courses, I would have started college as at least a sophomore. The only thing that kept me from getting my refund and taking myself back to the less risky path of finishing high school was a healthy apprehension of failure.

People in my hometown made such a big deal about me starting college early that I ended up making the local news. Additionally, all my family and friends knew I was starting college early. So I knew if I flunked out or quit, that would have hurt my reputation and made it harder for me to get support from people later. Plus, failing at this opportunity could have made it harder for me to get into good colleges later. Wanting to avoid those very negative outcomes, I worked harder than I had ever worked to do exceptionally well.

Note that experiencing helpful apprehension does not always mean that you should not go through with an action. It does always mean that you must carefully and critically assess whether or not this decision is worthwhile. In situations where you find the risk is worth proceeding, proceed aware and with caution. Think of surgery; the risk of serious bodily harm is always present when undergoing a surgical procedure. Nevertheless, that risk should not stop you from engaging in life-saving treatments. The risk of death is always a possible outcome when a fireman or police officer responds to a 911 call. However, that risk is something that theses brave men and women in uniform accept.

Accepting the risk does not mean being blind to the danger. This is why firemen and police officers train constantly; when possible they want to minimize risk to themselves and others. Similarly, when reasonably possible, try to limit the risks to yourself and others caused by your decisions. If you have accepted the risk of being an athlete in an extreme sport, wear proper protective gear. If you decide to take risks in the world of business, have a savings and make sure to limit your legal liability when possible. When you engage in risk-mitigating measures, your apprehension will subside, if not disappear altogether.

Now let's talk about fear. When you find that your uneasiness is debilitating fear instead of helpful apprehension, how do you deal with it? Just by acknowledging that you are hesitating out of fear, you have already overcome the first step. You cannot conquer an enemy you will not face. Make no mistake; fear is the enemy of your success. Once you have acknowledged that you are afraid of something, you can work to overcome it.

Fear is our natural response to the unknown, in the same way holding your breath is the natural response to straining to lift something heavy. Think about it, nobody ever teaches you to hold your breath when you lift, yet everyone does it. Holding your breath is incredibly unhealthy and counterproductive when trying to exert yourself physically. Yet it feels comfortable to give into the impulse. This same logic applies to fear. We are not taught to fear the unknown, and it is counterproductive for us to do so. And just like an athlete is trained through the impulse to hold their breath, you can train yourself to work through your fear.

Think about your first experiences in a swimming pool. There are some people who are able to leap immediately into the deep end and either sink or swim. The sink-or-swim method of coping with fear is, essentially, to completely immerse yourself in whatever makes you afraid. Imagine someone who is afraid to leave their comfort zone. The sink-or-swim method of conquering that fear would be for them to move to a completely new area and acclimate themselves to it. This method has its benefits; the primary benefit is that it can result in you coming to accept your fear in a seemingly instantaneous manner.

However, this method for coping with fear has a major downside. In a sink-or-swim situation, if you swim, that is great, but there is always the possibility that you will become overwhelmed and sink. Using the previous example, if the person moves to a new area and conquers their fears, the method is a success. Conversely, if they fail to conquer their fears, they will be stuck with a lease or mortgage in a place that makes them miserable. As such, I would only recommend this immersive approach when you are dealing with extreme time sensitivity or an opportunity that might only come once or twice in a lifetime. If that is the case throw yourself into the "deep end" and fight through your fear.

> "Life opens up opportunities to you, and you either take them or you stay afraid of taking them."
> Jim Carrey

A practical example of me engaging in the sink-or-swim method of conquering my fears would have been my first job out of law school. I was hired to be Assistant General Counsel for a pharmaceutical company based in Texas. I was going to be responsible for all day-to-day legal matters for the company. The idea was terrifying. If I screwed something up, hundreds of people's livelihoods could be impacted, millions of dollars could be lost, and, because we were making pharmaceuticals to combat pandemics, lives could be lost. There was nothing that I had done in law school that truly prepared me for this level of responsibility. To make matters worse, I was in school full time working on my Ph.D.

There were some aspects of accepting this job that gave me reasonable apprehension. I addressed those circumstances to the best of my ability and still felt uneasy. That is when it became apparent that I was just afraid. Still, this was truly a once in a lifetime opportunity that lawyers typically don't get unless they have been practicing law for at least a decade. Knowing that information, declining or delaying this opportunity was not an option. Despite my fear, I accepted the position.

When using the "sink-or-swim" method, you overcome fear by being too busy to think about being afraid. For me, I didn't have time to be afraid because I was too busy managing my company's legal department and doing my part to get us acquired by an international corporation. All while being in school full time. I didn't think about how afraid I should have been until I was explaining my job to somebody at the banquet celebrating our company's acquisition. At which point, the job was no longer terrifying because I had already been doing it for over a year.

A more practical approach to learning how to cope with fear is the way that most of us learned how to swim, in an incremental fashion. Typically, you are taught how to swim by spending a day getting comfortable floating in the water, then working on your kicking the next day and working on your arm movements the day after that. You continue to learn small lessons that, when put together, result in you swimming. Do the same thing with your other goals. Each day pick a couple of very manageable tasks to complete that puts you a few steps closer to achieving your goals.

For example, if your goal is to start a bakery, the prospect of actually starting a business might be too daunting. So instead set smaller incremental goals. Commit to look up three possible locations each day, or commit to practice & refine a recipe a day. After you get more confident, set a more aggressive interim goal like winning a baking competition. The objective is to make sure that every day you keep progressing through small steps that perpetually push you towards your goals. As you progress closer and closer to a goal, the tasks you chose will get bigger and bigger.

For this exercise, the plan you created in the previous chapters will be helpful. It will give you a roadmap of smaller incremental goals that you can work towards. In that detailed plan, find something that you are not afraid to do and do it. Do the same thing the next day, and the next day. Make sure that every day you accomplish a step towards your goal. Keep progressing a day at a time until your fear subsides.

Chapter 7:
Be Flexible but Uncompromising

Now that you have a plan that you are working, be mindful that your plan is not set in stone. As you learn more and do more, you should periodically revise your plan. As previously discussed, your plan is a living document, which means it should consume information, expand, and adapt to changing circumstance. This requires you to be flexible in your planning. However, you should NEVER compromise your core ideals.

Life is too unpredictable. No matter how good of a planner you are there will always be the contingency you don't account for. In engineering, we call this the N+1 Rule. Which essentially says that every system, no matter how well designed, has a situation or error that had not been previously thought of. Therefore, the success of any system, or in this case plan, will not be based on how well it can respond to planned occurrences. Success will be determined by how well it can adapt to unplanned situations.

When I began my academic journey, my plan was to get a medical degree so that I could conduct medical research. As I progressed through school I realized something about myself I didn't know; I hate hospitals with a passion! I love the work that is done in them, and I think that healing people is one of the noblest pursuits someone can undertake. Nevertheless, my spirit sinks a little whenever I set foot in a hospital.

> "Adapt what is useful, reject what is useless, and add what is specifically your own."
> Bruce Lee

Hating to stand in a hospital is a horrible trait for a medical student. Had adhered to my original plan, I would have spent years dreading the simple act of going to class. Imagine trying to manage the natural anxiety of taking a test, while being irritated by the entirety of your surroundings. Needless to say, this was an unexpected circumstance that could have derailed my progress. How did I cope? I was flexible and changed my plan up to exclude a medical degree.

That did not mean that I gave up on my desire to perform medical research. I kept the spirit of my goal in mind while changing my plan. Instead of pursuing a mechanical or electrical engineering degree in undergrad, I added a bioengineering degree to my plan. By majoring in bioengineering I was able to do quite a bit of medical research in undergrad.

Whenever you make changes to your plan, make sure that you keep the core values of your pursuits. In this context, I was flexible enough to change my pursuits to something else in the medical field. However, I did not compromise my desire to help people, improve health, and gain the title of doctor.

Also, despite the foreboding tone of the beginning of this chapter, life can be unexpectedly good. Do not be so fixated on completing your plan that you miss opportunities to achieve your major goals and dream. Remember your core values, motivations and dreams, and take opportunities that allow you to get closer to these desires.

For example, let's say that you are someone that has the dream of becoming a CEO. As part of this dream, you have set the goals of becoming a department manager, a district manager, a regional manager, a vice president, and a Chief Operating Officer (COO). By now, you have laid out a detailed plan on how you are going to accomplish each of those tasks, and you are working that plan. After a few years of being a stellar department manager, one of your product lines becomes the biggest product in the company. As a result of this success, you are given the opportunity to be a special assistant to your company's Chief Technology Officer (CTO); a position that reports directly to the CEO. What do you do? This seems like a no-brainer, you take the job. Yet, a lot of us, when confronted with these kinds of unexpected opportunities hesitate. Or we shy away from them altogether to try to preserve the plan. Be open to accepting unexpected opportunities.

This does not mean pursue any opportunity that you are given. Some opportunities are detours rather than shortcuts. In general, be open to unexpected opportunities if they help you get closer to your dream (e.g. a shortcut). To assess the difference between a detour and a shortcut, you must ask yourself two simple questions, "Does this opportunity lead me further from my dream?" and "Does this opportunity lead me closer to my dream or one of my major goals?"

Why is it important to ask both questions? Aren't they the same question? No, the questions are unique and equally as important. Anything that you know will actively take you further away from your dream is something that you should not do. So if the answer to the first question is "Yes," then this opportunity is a detour. What does it mean when the answer to the first questions is "No?" That depends on the second question. When the answer to the second question is "Yes," then this is an unexpected shortcut. Use the methods we discussed in the chapter about creating a plan to make a new plan that includes this unexpected opportunity. If the answers to both questions are, "No," then this is neither a shortcut nor a detour. This is a third category of unexpected opportunities called a time-sink.

Time-sinks are innocuous activities that neither benefit nor harm your progress. The problem is, as the name implies, they waste time! Typically, time-sinks are things that should be avoided, unless they are part of your reward system. We will discuss reward systems in later chapters.

When deciding whether something is a shortcut, detour, or time-sink, keep relationship-building in mind. I want to caution you against, dismissing opportunities because the benefit to yourself is not immediately apparent. Even if the opportunity itself does not necessarily get you closer to your goal, it may get you "relationship capital" with people who can help you achieve your goals. We will talk later about establishing a solid team. That is where we will talk in greater detail about relationship capital, and team members (e.g. coaches, mentors, sponsors, & cheerleaders). Nevertheless, if a trusted sponsor or mentor presents you with an opportunity or asks you to do something, strongly consider it before turning them down.

This is not an exact science, and definitely something that you will learn with time. In my first summer in law school, I worked for a major law firm in their intellectual property department. The head of that practice area was trying to grow the department and was looking for new lawyers to help him with that expansion. He was excited to bring me on board and "show me the ropes." This attorney was someone who could have been a solid mentor and potential sponsor (i.e. someone to give me access to high-level opportunities). I, being the naïve 20-year-old that I was at the time, did not yet know the importance of networking events. So I worked late and skipped social events that would have allowed me to get to know him better, and meet more of my potential clients and coworkers. The events that I skipped included one that he hosted at his home.

These networking events were not required or necessary for my job. They did not lead me closer to or further from my goals, which essentially made them a time-sink. Was it a wise decision for me to skip those networking events?

NO! Although the events were not directly beneficial, they were also not harmful. Had I gone, I would have built relationship capital with several potential mentors and could have gained a great sponsor. Those relationships could have been invaluable resources that helped me achieve my goals. For that reason alone, skipping those events was an example of a missed opportunity.

What were the consequences of missing these opportunities? First, I conveyed to my mentor/sponsor that I didn't really want his guidance. Next, it conveyed to the rest of my coworkers that I was not serious about advancement in the organization. And ultimately those perceptions cost me an opportunity to work with that organization the following summer. Working with them further could have been a shortcut to achieving some of my other goals. Thus, skipping those networking events was an example of a potential shortcut that I missed out on.

Conversely, while I was in my Ph.D. program, one of my advisors presented me with a research opportunity. It was a large multifaceted research project where I would work with a national team. This project could have lasted for years and resulted in multiple publications. In some regards, it was a great opportunity for me to get my name out there more.

However, my goal was not to acquire notoriety or more publications. My primary goal was to graduate in a timely fashion. My dream was to get a Ph.D. before my 26th birthday, and I had begun my program shortly after my 23rd birthday. Furthermore, the longer I was in school, the longer I would be accruing interest on my law school loans and the longer I would have to delay making income. If I took advantage of this opportunity, it is likely that the advisor would have wanted me to finish this research project before allowing me to graduate. Despite how much of an opportunity this research project could have been, it ultimately took me further away from my goals and dream. Thus, I made the correct decision in turning it down.

This was clearly the correct decision for me to make. Still, it would be foolish to expect that the decision would have no impact on my relationship with my advisor. Anytime you tell someone "no" you risk damaging your relationship with them. I understood that risk even before I made the decision. So not only did I have to decide that that project was something I could succeed without, I also had to decide that that advisor was somebody that I could survive having a damaged relationship with. My assessment was that potentially damaging my relationship with this particular advisor would do less to delay my graduation than participating in this extensive research project. I did not make that decision lightly. And even though it was the correct decision, my relationship with that advisor was still irreparably harmed.

The main point of the chapter is that plans can be fluid as long as you do not compromise yourself or your dreams. Once you internalize that you can change your plans, there is another added benefit. By internalizing the fact that you have the ability to change your mind, you become more comfortable starting to build towards your dreams and accomplishments. The previous chapter talked about analysis paralysis, and how one major cause is the belief that you can create the perfect plan. Thus part of the reason that we get caught in analysis paralysis is that we assign undue weight to our early decision making. In other words, we put the sole weight of our future actions and decisions on our current selves, which is an unreasonable pressure. Just because you make choices like your field, career, or industry does not mean that you can't choose something else later. When you realize this fact, you remove some of the undue pressure of early planning and are more willing to start working towards your dreams.

> "It takes many good deeds to build a good reputation, and only one bad one to lose it."
> Benjamin Franklin

We talk a lot about not compromising your dreams and making sure to keep focused on your destination even when the route changes. Be flexible but don't compromise, has another important meaning. Similar to how your plan can be challenged by unexpected circumstance, you and your character will be tested in the most unpredictable ways. We talk more about the value of your reputation in other sections, but it is a point worth reiterating.

Understand that "A good name is more desirable than great riches; to be esteemed is better than silver or gold." (Prov. 22:1 NIV) The reason your reputation is so valuable is because it can be converted into tangible resources & opportunities but money cannot buy a good reputation.

How can your reputation be converted into tangible resources? Every time someone gives you a loan, helps you develop an idea, or recommends you for an opportunity, that is your reputation being converted into something tangible. A concrete example of this phenomenon is fiat currency (e.g. paper money).

What is the intrinsic value of a $100 bill? Sounds like a stupid question, right? Let me rephrase it, how much would you pay for less than a gram of a cotton, linen and polymer blend that is dyed various colors of green? A $100-bill has no intrinsic value; the value of fiat money is the reputation of the country that is backing it. You exchange goods and services for worthless pieces of paper because you believe in the reputation of the country issuing them.

Similarly, your words have no intrinsic value. Saying "I will pay you back," or "I will owe you one," is not valuable to someone, unless a strong reputation is backing it. When backed by a good reputation, those words can literally be worth millions of dollars to someone. For this reason, a good reputation is the most valuable thing that you have.

For this reason, you should never compromise your principles or integrity to attain a shortcut to your dreams or goals. There are numerous paths to get to your goals, but a ruined reputation is nearly impossible to reestablish.

We can think of dozens of people who have attained short-lived fame and fortune based on cheap gimmicks, selling out their communities & families and prostituting themselves (both figuratively and literally) to get a few minutes in the spotlight. When you read that last sentence, you probably thought of a few who fall into that category. The thing that most of those people have in common is that they are neither famous nor fortunate right now. Keep that in mind when making decisions about your future.

Once your integrity has been called into question or your reputation is tarnished, you will never completely get the stain out. I cannot emphasize enough the importance of staying true to your personal ideals. Even when it is inconvenient or you think nobody is paying attention, integrity is a major key to long-term success. The main reason is that, no matter how good you perceive your ability to hide is, what is done in darkness has a tendency to come to light at some point. And once you lose your reputation, it is almost impossible to get it back.

A test that I use to see whether or not I should avoid doing something is to ask the following questions:

"Could I justify this to my 10-year-old self?"

"Could I justify this to my mom?"

"Will I be able to justify this to God on my day of judgment?"

And *"Would all three approve?"*

If I can honestly answer yes to all four of those questions, then I know that I am behaving with integrity. You should strongly reconsider your actions if you are ever considering a course of action that does not allow you to honestly answer all these questions with a "Yes!"

Chapter 8:
Delayed Gratification

Delayed gratification is the act of not giving yourself or allowing yourself to have something until it is the most beneficial and least costly. Another way of looking at it is you resist the temptation to attain smaller more immediate rewards so that you may attain a greater reward later. I have found that I am able to get so much more from life when I am willing to be patient. Delayed gratification is a tool that will allow you to have and accomplish more in life, but it isn't always an easy tool to master. There are three pitfalls that make delayed gratification difficult.

In order to properly utilize delayed gratification, the first pitfall to avoid is mistaking things that you want for things that you need. How many times have you told yourself "I need a new [blank]?" Whether it is a nicer phone, a newer car, new shoes, or more money, we are quick to categorize something as a need. When we do that, we send the message to ourselves that we must get this thing at any cost or else our survival will be threatened. How often is that actually true?

Ultimately, there are very few things that you need to survive: food, water, shelter, health, and safety. Unless something, in a very direct fashion, affects your ability to acquire one of these things for yourself or your family, it is a "want" and not a "need." Sometimes it is hard to distinguish between the two. When determining whether or not something is a need, ask the questions, "If I do not have this will it negatively impact my or my family's ability to live, be healthy or be safe?" If the answer is no, it is something you want and not something you need.

The reason that this distinction is important is because wants can be delayed, needs cannot. Thus, by correctly differentiating between what you need and what you want, you can more efficiently use your time, energy, and money. As a rule, you never want to spend too much time, energy, or money on what you want and not have enough of one of those resources remaining to get everything you actually need.

Sometimes that rule can result in some tough decisions. When I say "want" versus "need," the first things people think about are situations like buying new shoes versus paying your rent. Those are the easy decisions, but sometimes differentiating between a need and a want can be tough. If you are like me, you feel a "need to help others." Although it is valiant to help others, there is a reason that airlines tell you to put on your oxygen mask before assisting others. Let's say you try to assist someone else with their mask, but you faint during the process because of a lack of oxygen. Now, you won't be able to ensure that the person's mask is secured AND you won't have anybody to assist with your mask. By failing to prioritize your need for oxygen, you actually put both of you in a worse situation.

During the finals' week of my 4th year of college, I spent so much of my energy and time tutoring other people. My rationale was that my test was on the last day of finals' week, and they needed my help. When I got everybody through their tests, I barely had any energy left for my own test. I needed to do well in that class and wanted to help my friends with their finals as well. But because I thought I "needed" to help them, I didn't have enough time or energy to get through the studying I needed to do.

What would have happened if I hadn't passed that class? It could have delayed my graduation from undergrad and harmed my ability to get into law school. I would have had to take a greater course load to make up for the failed class and bring my Grade Point Average (GPA) back up. In which case, the next semesters I would not have had time to do as much tutoring and peer mentoring. Thus, I would have been less able to help people in the future and be further from achieving my dream. Luckily, even though I bombed that exam, I had done very well throughout the rest of the semester. Despite my final exam grade, I did well enough to make it out of that class with my GPA intact.

It is important to realize that not everything you want is selfish, or petty. You can want some pretty great things! I want to contribute positively to world health and the education of young people. But if I don't prioritize being healthy and well educated how can I heal or educate others. By addressing my needs first, I ensure that I have the ability to address the needs of others. Similarly, you may want to do some great things, but make sure that you are not neglecting your needs in the process.

The second pitfall to avoid is failing to realize the difference between delayed gratification and deprivation. We often times think of "delayed gratification" as if it is us telling ourselves "maybe later," which is adult-speak for "never." We believe that if we don't get something now we just won't get it; thus, we adopt the "now or never" mentality. Saying "maybe later" is not delayed gratification; that is essentially deprivation. Delayed gratification means that at some point you are going to get the thing that you want, but you are going to wait until the cost is less substantial. Therefore, it is not a "maybe later." Delayed gratification means that you are telling yourself "definitely later!"

I do not believe that it is necessary to lead a deprived life. I fully expect to have everything that I have dreamed about having, and do all the stuff I have dreamed about doing. I have a nice list of achievements I plan to make, places I plan to travel, and

> "There are still many causes worth sacrificing for, so much history yet to be made"
> Michelle Obama

adventures I will have. Rest assured that I am slowly but surely checking items off of that list. You should expect to, within reason, have the things you want. The point of delayed gratification is to sacrifice a bit now so that you can have a lot later.

I love movies of all kinds, comedies, action, anime, westerns, sports movies, biopics, etc.; when I was in Jr. High, I made a list of movies and television shows that I wanted to own. This was prior to the existence of live streaming, and the prevalence of online portals. So if I wanted to see movies I had to rent or own them, and for some of the television box sets, renting was not an option. At the time, I didn't have a lot of money, and some of the box sets on my list were hundreds of dollars. Nevertheless, over the course of the next 8 years, I systematically acquired all of the items on my list (plus a lot more). By waiting some of the box sets became significantly less expensive to own, and I gave myself time to get better jobs and save more money. Even though the process took years, I made sure that I got what I wanted. It doesn't need to take that long every time. Sometimes it can be as simple as waiting a few months for the beta version of a new device, or the year-end clearance event for a new car. The most important thing to remember is that you are delaying not depriving.

This brings me to the last pitfall to avoid. The main reason so many of us believe that delayed gratification means deprivation is because we don't make a plan to get what we want. You can't expect that if you don't have the funds for a nicer new car today, that without any additional effort or forethought you are going to have that money sometime in the future. Similarly, you are not going to get that degree in the future if you aren't even enrolled in classes or making a plan to be enrolled in classes now. If you want delayed gratification to work, use the steps in this book to make a plan so that you know how the delay will be beneficial. Clearly articulate and understand how you will get to what you want at a lower personal cost. Turn those wants into short-term goals. Yes, the focus of this book is heavily geared towards giving you the tools to achieve major dreams, but the same tools apply to achieving short-term goals as well.

Using the example of the list of movies and television shows that I wanted, I developed a plan for how I would acquire more money to be able to buy them. Additionally, I kept a continuous watch on when the prices were coming down on items on my list. Over the course of that 8 year period, I made sure that I continually progressed towards my goal. By the time I acquired the last item on my list, it had reduced in price from over $120 to less than $30.

I was only willing to wait that long because I had a plan in place to assure myself that one day I would complete my list. Without that plan, delaying gratification would have been more difficult, and I might have prioritized these wants over my needs. I could have easily blown several paychecks acquiring these movies & TV shows, which may have left me unable to get everything that I needed.

Exercising the discipline to delay gratification does not just apply to getting things you want; it can also be applied to your long-term goals. Anything worth having in life is going to require some sacrifices. Nothing in life is free, and you will either pay for it now or later. Anybody you see "living it up" and having a great time in life is either cashing in an investment or running up a bill. So it is up to you to decide if you want to put in the work now and spend the rest of your life reaping the benefits, or have all of your fun now and spend the rest of your life working off that debt.

> "Discipline is just choosing between what you want now and what you want most"

During the time that you are working to acquire necessary education or skills so that you can maximize your salary, you will have peers who are out having fun. When you are paying dues so that you can move up the ranks in your company, there will be concerts, events, and other exciting activities that you miss.

When you are unwilling to delay gratification, you either accomplish less or each accomplishment cost you more. Think about our building metaphor. If you have ever had the great pleasure (or misfortune) of having to hire a contractor to do work on a building, you have likely seen the "Contractor Triangle." It is a triangle labeled with Quality, Cost and Time. Typically, your contractor will use it as a tool to level set your expectations about how long a job is going to take or how much it is going to cost. The idea is that you can have any two sides of the triangle but you cannot have all three. This means that a job can be done at a high quality and a low price, but it will take a long time; a job can be done at a high quality and quickly, but it is going to be very expensive; or a job can be done quickly at a low cost, but will be low quality.

This same principle applies to building towards great accomplishments. In the context of your life, you can either chose to have lower quality achievements, sacrifice time, or pay a costly price for attaining your goals. Take, for example, the goal of earning a large sum of money. If you adhere to the principle of delayed gratification, you take a bit longer to gather the education and training needed to establish an extraordinarily lucrative career or a profitable business. By taking the time to put in the work in a proactive fashion, it may take you a bit longer to start making significant money, but when you do, the large sum of money you make will be measured in hundreds of thousands or millions.

Conversely, if you decide that you want to make that same amount of money but don't want to invest the time, the money becomes more costly. What does that mean; how can money cost more? The first way in which money can cost more is your reputation. There are few things that you have that are innately valuable and irreplaceable once lost. Time is one of them; another is your reputation. There are numerous unsavory manners to make money quickly. You can lie, cheat, steal, and do any number of things that devalue your worth as a human being. However, when you go down the path of chasing quick money in unscrupulous manners, the cost to your reputation is something that you can never recover. This doesn't just apply to making money; other examples include athletes who are caught cheating, people who plagiarize other's work, artists knowingly putting out low-quality work and companies who knowingly sell unsafe products to increase short-term profitability. Whether you call it lost goodwill, being disgraced, or simply disappointing people, it is all the same thing. You pay with your reputation when you chase quick unscrupulous shortcuts to success.

The other way in which money can cost more is preventing you from making more money in the future. A perfect example of this is if attempting to make money quickly results in you doing something illegal. At the point that you are discovered, arrested and/or fired, you are going to find it hard to find a job in the future. Think of examples when a person's or organization's reputation is harmed. How many millions did the cyclists in those doping scandals lose? What happened to the careers of singers after lip-syncing scandals? What happens to hedge fund managers after a Ponzi scheme is discovered? In all of these cases, the person will get some quick money, but afterward, they risk having their money taken away and never being able to make money again.

The last possible configuration of the Contractor Triangle is accomplishments that are quick and inexpensive. These are the accomplishments that you aim for when you are not very aggressive in setting lofty goals or pursuing big dreams. In the example of acquiring money, this would be making money in a way that doesn't take much time or harm your reputation. It is okay to have some goals that you set that fall into this category. Practically speaking, not every one of your goals is going to be on the scale of Dr. King's dream. However, goals like this should be used to get you to bigger accomplishments. So maybe you only need a couple hundred dollars to pay for books one semester, or you just need to save up enough to get a reliable car for your morning commute. As previously stated, the exercises and principles in the book can be applied to short-term goals as well as long-term dreams. Just make sure that all of your goals and dreams are not this type of short-term accomplishments.

Whether it is going to get more training before you enter the workforce, holding off on buying your dream car or prioritizing addressing your needs so that you are able to better serve others, delayed gratification is an effective tool that will allow you to get more from life.

Chapter 9:
Celebrate EVERY Victory

Part of your planning process needs to include a rewards system; this is a plan to celebrate your accomplishments big and small. Why is this important? We talked a lot about motivation in previous chapters. You should know why you do the things you do and be heavily motivated by that rationale. However, sometimes it is hard to mentally make a direct connection between what you need to do on a daily or weekly basis and your overall motivations. In those moments, your reward system will give you the motivation you need to accomplish your daily, weekly and monthly goals.

Let us use the example of preparing for a weekly meeting with a boss or advisor. To prepare for this meeting you need to review material and prepare a presentation. Now, bombing one meeting is unlikely to have a significant impact on accomplishing your dreams. As such, the big motivations that drive you to want to achieve your ambitions may fail you when preparing for your weekly meetings. Why is this a problem? It is true that, typically, messing up one weekly meeting, or one test, or one homework assignment will not have a long-term impact on your success. However, where do you draw the line? What happens when that one, becomes two, or three, or a dozen? Furthermore, what if that one meeting you didn't prepare for was the tipping point of a decision to promote, or that one test was the difference between passing and failing?

Ultimately, you never know when you are going to get a golden opportunity to jump-start your dreams. Tyrese Gibson went from being a no-name model to an internationally known recording artist and actor because he gave his all singing in a Coca Cola commercial. There were times when I have given speeches in front of small audiences that led to my most lucrative speaking engagements. I have had what I thought were casual meetings that quickly turned into job interviews. Put simply, "If you stay ready you don't have to get ready." You always have to push yourself to be ready because you never know when opportunity will knock.

It is easy to tell you to always be prepared, but it is often easier said than done. How do you get past those times when you really don't feel like getting off of a full day of work or classes only to continue to work at home? You cannot rely solely on knowing what drives you to get you through all of the day-to-day tasks. In order to do that, you must set up a rewards system.

Make sure that every accomplishment, big or small, has a corresponding reward that you can look forward to. For example, I have always loved movies. I think it was because some of my earliest memories were going to the

> "The more you praise and celebrate your life, the more there is in life to celebrate"
> Oprah Winfrey

movie theater with my family. We would go to the dollar movie theater to see a few movies and then go across the street to an arcade. For that reason, I would watch a movie after every test that I took in college. And after a successfully completed semester, I would get some Rocky-Road ice cream and have a movie marathon.

Make your reward something you actually look forward to. Whether it is eating at your favorite restaurant after successfully getting through your quarterly report, or watching your favorite show after you successfully finish your weekly report, you should have something to look forward to after small victories.

When setting up a reward system for yourself there are only three rules: 1. Celebrate the completion not the result, 2. Make sure the celebration recharges you and 3. Make sure the celebration is proportionate to the accomplishment.

The first and most important rule of rewarding your victories is that your reward should not be contingent on the outcome. The victory is not the result; the victory is working your best to get through a task. Regardless of the result, you have achieved something just by working through your plan and hitting whatever milestone you have set for yourself.

Often times, we feel like we are only deserving of a reward when we achieve the outcome we hoped for. What we are really telling ourselves is that we are only worthy of a reward when someone else gives you approval. Thus, we do not reward ourselves unless we get a good grade, a promotion, or win a competition. That puts the source of your motivation in the hands of someone else, and you never want others to have control over your psyche.

We have already discussed why motivations that are dependent on someone else are less effective. The same principle applies to your personal reward system. If the only time you reward yourself is when you receive the approval of someone else, then you are going to be less motivated to try when the outcome is uncertain. And even worse, if you are certain that you won't get the approval you need, your reward system is rendered useless. There are times when I had to work tirelessly knowing that the likely outcome was going to be a form of failure.

Why work hard when you know that you are probably going to fail? First and foremost, it is impossible to truly fail until you give up. Every unfavorable outcome that happens before you give up is just a temporary setback. Additionally, no matter how certain you are that you are "going to fail," you never truly know the outcome. And the only way that you are going to snatch victory from the jaws of a near-certain defeat is by working to the best of your ability. Your reward system is what helps you do that, even when circumstances seem bleak.

I remember one of the most trying days of my life. I was working with a group on a medical device that could measure the heart and breathing rate of small infants. It was the night before a big presentation, and our prototype was not working. Over the course of that night, my entire team disappeared one by one, leaving me alone to finish the design. I worked so long, that I got to see the sunrise from my lab desk. Still, when I left the lab, our prototype was fully functional with 10 hours to spare. I went home to get some much-deserved rest. But my sleep was interrupted by my phone ringing continually a couple hours later.

One of my group members had the bright idea that the circuit I built was not "pretty enough." So they removed all of the wires I had painstakingly put together to form this complex network of circuits, made them prettier and tried to put them back together. I am sure that you can see where this is going. They could not reconstruct my circuit. With less than 7 hours until the demonstration and less than 3 hours of sleep, I had to find a way to do what took me 3 days to figure out. I committed to myself that I was going to work tirelessly for the entire 7 hours, and regardless of how horribly it turned out, I was taking a long, coma-like nap with no phone, watching multiple movies and getting some Rocky-Road ice cream.

The mental, physical, and emotional fatigue of this ordeal started to seriously take its toll. Nevertheless, my group mates left me by myself in the lab, again. Eventually, I started bargaining with myself, thinking things like, "Maybe bombing this demonstration wouldn't get me too far off track from my goals. It is just one demonstration in a year-long project." When those thoughts crept into my mind, I reminded myself about my reward system. If I didn't work through all 7 hours, then I wouldn't get the rewards I promised myself.

Of course, it was impossible for me to duplicate what I had built over the course of several days in a few drowsy hours. However, because I kept working, I figured out a shortcut to repairing the prototype to perform just well enough to get through the demonstration. Although it wasn't up to the standard I would have liked, it was more than enough to get the approval for the next phase of design.

In this circumstance, I was going to get my reward regardless of how things turned out, but only if I worked hard for the entire time. Because I was motivated to work hard, I was pleasantly surprised by the outcome. Still, even if it had turned out less than successful, as I had expected, I would have given myself the same rewards.

Along with being contingent on completion instead of outcome, your reward system must actually make you feel recharged. Much like your motivation, it has to be personal to you. Your reward should be something that legitimately lifts your spirits AND appropriately refreshes you. That "and" is important.

Being appropriately refreshed means having your energy restored with enough time to begin whatever your next task is. If this task is the last thing you have to do before taking an extended vacation, then almost anything you like doing can be refreshing. However, if you have to do your next task the next day, then you have to be more selective about your reward. Let's say you are somebody who loves to play basketball. Yes, playing basketball might lift your spirits. But if every time you play you end up needing to sit in Epson salt and are bed ridden for a day, it is not something that appropriately refreshes you in this context. When your next task is within a day or two of your last task, playing basketball may not a good reward for you.

Conversely, if you are somebody who loves sweets, ice cream might be very refreshing for you. However, if you are also on a diet and are going to feel guilty about eating ice cream, then it isn't something that is going to lift your spirits. As such, ice cream probably wouldn't be a good reward for you.

"Zombieland Rule #32 Enjoy the little things"

Your rewards can be anything you choose. You can go to a party, buy yourself a gift, go out to eat, cook yourself something special, or go take a trip. It can be as simple as getting yourself a Twinkie, or as big as going to see your favorite artist in concert. You can have it be something that you do solo, or if you are a social person, it can be meeting up with some friends you haven't seen in a while. As long as your reward lifts your spirits and appropriately refreshes you, it is completely up to you.

However, one caveat is that your reward should not be a necessity. In cases where you are rewarding yourself with a necessity, you have developed a punishment system. What does that mean? If your reward to yourself is anything that falls within Maslow's Hierarchy of Needs (food, water, shelter, etc.), you are not rewarding yourself for completing a task. You are punishing yourself if you do not complete your task. In other words, your reward to yourself should never be the avoidance of harm to yourself, because that is a system that relies on punishment which is not as effective.

What are examples of punishment systems? There are the extreme versions of punishment based systems like "If I finish this book tonight I won't make myself run bleachers tomorrow." Or, "If I finish this report I won't flog myself." But I would pray that none of you would do that to yourself. The thing you have to be careful about is a more subtle version of punishment systems. "If I finish studying this, then I will let myself go to sleep." Or "when I get through this presentation without stumbling, I will go get dinner." In reality, you are not rewarding yourself, you are saying if you fail you don't get to sleep or eat respectively.

Compare this to a true reward system. "If I finish studying this, then I will let myself sleep in an extra two hours." Or "when I get through this presentation without stumbling, I will get a cupcake to go with my dinner." Reward systems are about giving yourself something extra you wouldn't normally receive.

The reason you don't want to set up a punishment based system for yourself is because it is harder to maintain and can make you resentful. Punishment based systems only work when the person giving the punishment is not the same person receiving it. In order for this short-term motivation system to work, you have to have consistency. If the person implementing your punishment is yourself, you are inevitably going to give yourself mercy. Thus, you will not consistently follow through with your threats, and the motivation factor reduces.

On the off chance that you are consistent with your punishments, you are going to become resentful. Whenever you are being punished you resent your punisher; that is human nature. Think about how often we hear of people threatening their judge or prosecutor in a criminal case. In this case, you are the one punishing yourself. Even worse, you are creating a mental correlation between the accomplishment of your dream and being punished. It will not be long until you associate the pain of your punishment with your dream and resent the dream itself. For these reasons, rewards systems are a far more effective tool for driving you to success.

The last requirement of a reward system is that it be proportional to the accomplishment. This has been implied throughout the chapter, but I wanted to make it unequivocally clear. Do not be somebody who rewards yourself with a TV show for every page you read. Your rewards system is not a license to perpetually indulge in distractions. The reward should correspond to a legitimate task completion and major milestones. If you want your reward to be a 30 minute TV show, make that be a reward for reading an entire chapter. Or if you want to be rewarded per page, make the reward be one of your favorite chips and eat a Dorito every time you turn a page. But the work should take longer than the reward.

For some people, their issue is using a reward system as an excuse to indulge in distractions, but others have the exact opposite problem. Your reward for completing a 4-year-journey should not be a cupcake. After every one of my graduations, I celebrated with a party and a trip somewhere. Understand that celebrating your milestones is a necessary part of achieving success, and should be done even when it isn't convenient.

The week after I graduated law school I had to start studying for the bar exam for three months and the week after finishing the bar exam I started my Ph.D. program. I had no time to properly celebrate this milestone, so I was creative in finding time for my trip and my party. Since I didn't have time for a trip after graduation, I took it before graduation. The day after finishing finals I flew to Los Angeles to see one of my favorite artists in concert. Then I waited until a month into my Ph.D. program to celebrate with my family and friends. Remember, delayed gratification is an effective tool to maximize your time.

> "Life ain't no dress rehearsal."
> Bernie Mac

If you don't make time to celebrate your victories, big and small, with an appropriate reward, you will burn out before you reach your dream. So many people think that success means working endlessly. Yes, hard work is a necessity to succeed in life, but so are rest, relaxation, and fun. Although this almost two-decade long journey has been challenging, I have found ways to have fun at every stage. The fun times reenergizes you for the difficult segments of your journey. As such, it is important that you find ways to enjoy the journey towards your dream. Your reward system will ensure that you do that.

Once you have developed your reward system; make sure to periodically update it. The more you do things the better you get at them and the more effortless they become. Maybe the first few months of having to prepare a weekly report were difficult for you, but now it takes you less than 20 minutes to complete. Update the reward criteria to reflect your new ability. So maybe you give yourself the same reward for completing a month's worth the weekly reports that you used to give yourself weekly. Or maybe you find a new challenge to reward. Make sure that your reward system remains proportional to your effort.

Also, update your rewards as your tastes change. As I have mentioned before, I used to love Rocky-Road ice cream. I incorporated it heavily into my rewards system. However, as I got older, my taste buds have changed. Now, my sweet tooth just isn't as strong as it used to be. As such, a good steak has replaced Rocky-Road ice cream as my reward for a hard week.

As your tastes change, your rewards should change with them. This does not just apply to food; this rule also applies to activities. Maybe going to bars and parties is not as refreshing and uplifting for you as it used to be. You might also have found activities that you didn't even know you liked. For example, some of my friends from other states are surprised to find out how much they enjoy going to gun ranges. Periodically reevaluate the activities that comprise your rewards system.

The objective of establishing a system for rewarding your victories, both big and small, is to drive you to fully apply yourself to short-term goals. Your reward system can incentivize you to work hard in situations where your core motivation may not be sufficient.

Chapter 10:
Work Smart

Throughout this book, we have talked about working hard. Now, let's talk about working smart. Pairing working hard with working smart is a recipe for success.

The first method for working smart that I want to introduce is the concept of multitasking. We have largely talked about pursuing goals as if it is always a linear process. Each step has had one step that precedes it, and you can only do one thing at a time. To some extent, there will be parts of your journey that proceed in this kind of linear fashion. However, most of the time, you will have the option to multitask on some level. Effective use of multitasking can greatly increase the speed at which you progress towards your dream.

When I say multitasking, it may conjure a cartoonish image of a person doing a different task with each hand simultaneously. However, multitasking in this context does not necessarily mean doing multiple things simultaneously. Trying to do multiple complex activities at the same time is an impractical approach to most multitasking. In this context, a more accurate view of multitasking is beginning or resuming a new task before the current task is complete.

An example of multitasking in an industrial context is a team drilling for oil in a difficult area. When you are drilling deep, or through earth that is hard or inconsistent, there is a lot of possible problems that can arise. One of those problems is that your drill bit may unexpectedly break underground. When this happens, you will need a new drill bit. If the cause of the break was the unexpected characteristics of the ground that you are drilling in, you may need a new type of drill bit.

Depending on how rare this part is or if it needs to be custom fabricated, getting new drill bits in can take several days. During that time there are dozens of members of the drill team who can no longer drill for oil. While waiting for the new part to arrive, will those employees be sitting on their hands? No, time is money, and the team is going to try to maximize their time. An efficient drill team will perform diagnostic checks to ensure that nothing else breaks when drilling resumes, prepare the rig to install the new drill bit, and they may even get a head start on routine maintenance of the equipment. By doing so they reduce the total time it will take for them to complete the project and reach their goal. This method of multitasking is something that we often do at work, but are sometimes less willing to apply to our personal life.

Consider the example of wanting to start a business. If you treated your personal life like you treat projects at work, whenever you had downtime in one area of your life, you would apply that time to advancing your business. This means that, whenever you have additional time, you would perform tasks that get you closer to owning a business.

Unfortunately, this is not the way that most of us approach achieving our goals. Often times we will only work on one thing at a time. Rather than continuously working towards starting a business, you will start by dedicating yourself to school. Then once you complete school, you will dedicate yourself to getting more work experience. Then once you have gotten more work experience, you will start the background research to figure out your plan for starting a business. Working this way, instead of multitasking will result in you taking much longer to get to your destination, if at all. What you are doing in this context is creating false prerequisites to achieving your goal.

Multitasking is a useful tool, but in order to properly multitask, you have to have a clear vision of the complete plan. This is the reason why creating a plan is such an important part of the process. Returning to our building analogy; by having a framework established, you can build towards your goals more efficiently. Think about constructing a house. How do the builders progress through the project? Do they build each room to completion and then move onto the next room? No. Builders will have phases of the project and complete each phase for the entire home. So one day may be inserting insulation, one afternoon may be putting in drywall, and so on. Builders proceed through each phase until the construction project is complete. The reason that builders are able to do this is because the frame of the house lets them know where everything is going to be. Thus, builders are able to progress towards completion more quickly by multitasking and working on multiple areas of the structure simultaneously.

How would this work practically? If your goal is to own an automotive repair shop, you would need to learn about business and cars. In order to get that base level of knowledge, you could work to become an expert in cars and then go back to school to become an expert in all things business. That would be the equivalent of completing construction on one room before beginning construction on the next. Whereas, a more efficient way of doing things would be to work towards becoming an expert in auto repair while simultaneously taking supplemental classes or reviewing supplemental material to learn about business.

Multitasking is not always an option. There are some things that must be completed before others (i.e. prerequisite tasks). Part of the reason it is important to realize that multitasking is possible is so you actually take the time to learn the prerequisite tasks to your goals. Quite often, we assume what the prerequisite tasks are, and never actually take the time to test their necessity. Thus, we end up putting up artificial roadblocks to our success.

If there is not an unbreakable rule or a law that explicitly tells you something is a prerequisite to one of your goals or your dream, you are not required to complete it before proceeding to the next step. I want you to really internalize that statement. Unless there is a law or an unbreakable rule that tells you that you are required to do it before undertaking your goal or dream, you may multitask. The reason I reiterated that point is because most of us put artificial prerequisites on ourselves.

Here is an example of this principle. There is a law in each state of the United States that prevents you from practicing law without being properly licensed. These licensing boards require the completion of a law degree before you can receive this license. This is a rule that the licensing boards do not make exceptions for. The schools that issue these degrees strongly recommend that their students work at least a year or two before applying for admissions. Based on what I have told you, what are the prerequisite to practicing law in the United States?

Working for at least a year before getting a law degree and then becoming licensed, right? Although I agree that getting a law degree and becoming licensed are prerequisites, there was nothing that required you to work for a year. A lot of use hear phrases like "we strongly recommend," "we encourage," "we strongly discourage," "you should," and "it would be best if you," and interpret them as "you must." That is not the case.

I spent the majority of my life taking on challenges that I was "strongly recommended," to avoid. It was strongly recommended that I not start the 3rd grade at 6 years old. I was strongly discouraged from taking such a heavy course load my first year in college. I only made two B's that year; the rest of my grades were straight A's. When I was applying to law school, my prelaw advisor flat out told me to set my sights lower because he didn't believe that I was a strong enough candidate to get into a top 20 ranked school. I ignored that recommendation, got into and graduated from Harvard Law School. Most recently, I was strongly discouraged from taking such a rigorous Ph.D. curriculum. If I didn't take the time to clearly understand the difference between requirements and suggestions, I would have never reached the goal of graduating with my three degrees before the age of 26.

I am not suggesting for you to ignore wise counsel when it is given. I am saying that not all counsel given is wise. In these situations, none of the people offering me their "strong recommendations" and unsolicited advice were part of my team. Therefore, they had little understanding of my capabilities and no real understanding of my journey to that point. When confronted with a suggestion or recommendation that contradicted my trajectory, I would always consult my team. If my team agreed with the suggestion, I would add it in as an intermediary step. However, I would do so knowing that it was a choice that I could revisit if necessary and not a requirement.

In addition to effective multitasking, another method for working smart is to know the Point of Diminishing Returns. Typically, regardless of what you are working on, there is a strong correlation between the time you spend on something and an improved outcome. If you spend an extra 30 minutes on a presentation, then you are typically going to improve the quality of that presentation. Similarly, if you spend an extra hour on studying, you can reasonably expect to see an improvement on your grade. If you spend an extra day on product development, you are typically going to see a proportionate increase in product quality. All of this is typically true, except when you have hit a Point of Diminishing Returns.

What is the Point of Diminishing Returns? This is the point, after extensive work on a project or assignment has been performed, where the amount of time and effort you will have to put in to improve the results ceases to be possible or reasonable. Think about taking a test back in high school. The amount of effort you had to put in to get from a score of 0% to a score of 50% might be an hour, and to get from 50% to 70% it might take another hour. Maybe with another hour of studying your grade would increase from 70% to 90%. However, if you wanted to get a perfect score on your test, then you would have to know every obscure reference the teacher might have chosen from the material. So instead of taking another hour to get that perfect score, it took you an additional 2 hours to get from 90% to that perfect score of 100%. Was it worth it to almost double your study time to raise your grade from an A to a higher A? In most cases, the answer is no.

This premise is especially true if you are juggling multiple assignments at the same time. Using the test example, let's say that all tests operated on this same grade-to-study-time correlation. In the time it takes a student to study to get a perfect score in 2 exams that student could have finished studying to get an A on 3 exams. Keep in mind, studying for the perfect scores would not actually improve their GPA, and could hurt their GPA if they run out of time trying to study for the third exam. Thus, in this scenario, trying to study to get from 90% to 100% is an example of reaching (and exceeding) the Point of Diminishing Returns.

This same principle applies to everything that you do. Perfectionists are not the successful people in this world. The people who are most successful are the ones who realize that perfection is a pipe dream and consistently high quality is their standard. If you allow perfect to be the enemy of great and great to be the enemy of good, you will consistently be playing catch up and never have enough time to achieve your maximum capability.

There are some things in life with no margin for error. If you are a brain surgeon or a nuclear physicist, doing your job at only an (A-) level can cost people their lives. However, if you are a nuclear physicist, you do not need to waste time preparing your daily coffee with the same precision you conduct fission reactions. The purpose of identifying the Point of Diminishing Returns is to reduce the amount of time you spend on activities with lower importance. This allows you to have more time to dedicate to major tasks.

When you are pursuing lofty goals, time can be a resource you wish you had more of. Fortunately, you have been blessed with the same 24 hour day as everyone else. Working smart with universal time constraints directly impacts our ability to achieve our goals. Since there is no way to make days longer, the best way to gain more time is to most efficiently use the time you have. For me, effective multitasking and knowing the Point of Diminishing Returns has consistently allowed me to do more with seemingly less available time.

Chapter 11:
Finish What You Start

When I travel to high schools and universities around the country to speak, I pretty consistently ask one question, "What is the one thing you can get from a college that you can't get anywhere else?"

Typically, students will respond with things like "life experiences," "lifelong friendships," or "an education." All of these answers are wrong. Even without going to college, you can have plenty of the same life experiences. I met a good number of my lifelong friends in high school and through work. Additionally, with the availability of books and internet resources, you can surely get an education outside of college. The truth is, with the exception of one thing, all of what you get in college you can get somewhere else.

Eventually, if nobody guesses it, I will let them know the answer, "A college degree!" A college degree is the only thing you can get from college that you cannot get anywhere else. The point of this exercise is to show them something that I am hoping to show you: *There is a lot of value in finishing what you start.*

I recognize that a vast number of my readers are not going to be high school or college students. Nevertheless, I began this chapter with the example of college because it perfectly illustrates the message of this chapter. You derive the most value from college when you finish it. In most companies, there is not a substantial difference between the pay of a fulltime employee who has "Some College" over that of a fulltime employee who only has a high school diploma. Thus, if you go to college for the experience and without a plan to graduate with a worthwhile degree, then you are not capturing the value of college.

This is a reminder that the purpose of setting goals and working towards them is to finishing them. We have all heard the phrase "Almost Doesn't Count." That applies here as well. Almost accomplishing your goals or almost making your dream come true is not the purpose of this book. When utilizing this information, the objective is to complete all of your goals and achieve your dream.

Using the college example, we are going to examine some of the reasons people don't finish accomplishments that they start. The top reasons that I have seen for people not finishing college are: 1. No motivation, 2. No planning, 3. No delayed gratification, and 4. No interim checkpoints.

At this point in the book, you have the tools to overcome all of these pitfalls. A reoccurring theme in this book is that you will not achieve a goal that is not solidly grounded in your motivation. A lack of motivation creates a lack of consistency and follow-through. When your actions

> "Without commitment you'll never start. But without consistency, you'll never finish"
> Denzel Washington

are tied to something that drives you, you are more likely to put in consistent effort. As such, all of your goals and your dreams should be firmly grounded in one or more of your core motivations. When you do this, your motivation will make you feel uneasy and bothered if you ever get off track from your goals.

"If you fail to plan, you plan to fail." A person who doesn't have a clearly articulated plan for success has basically created a plan for failure. This emphasizes the importance of creating a plan. Remember that you plan should also include a planned reward system. Your reward system helps you stay driven when your core motivations are not enough.

Your plan will never be perfect. So once you have a workable plan, start building towards your dream. While working to accomplish your goals, you should update your plan to reflect changing circumstances and new information. Remember, as long as you are working your plan, you can avoid being distracted or derailed by detours.

Delayed gratification is a tool that allows you to achieve and gain more while it costs you less. If you are in a perpetual state of instant gratification, you are unable to properly invest in your future. Thus, you will have all of your benefits now and spend the rest of your life paying for them. With delayed gratification, you invest a bit of upfront work and reap the benefits of it for years to come.

Finally, we have already addressed the importance of intermediate milestones and celebrating those successes. A lot of time, people quit because they cannot see the "light at the end of the tunnel." The more ambitious and longer-term your dream is, the more difficult it will be to maintain motivation throughout your journey. To combat this, we talked about establishing milestone victories that you can celebrate along the way to making your dream a reality. This is a method for sustaining your motivation over longer periods of times.

The tools mentioned, along with the other information included herein, address what I have seen to be some of the largest barriers to success. However, no matter how many tools I give you, it is you who must decide to use them. I speak from personal experience when I say that if you apply these principles you can make your dreams come true. Nevertheless, these principles only work if you commit to pursuing your passions and never give up on your dreams. Commit to yourself that once you start this journey you will not give up until you finish!

> "Strength does not come from physical capacity. It comes from an indomitable will."
> Mahatma Gandhi

Chapter 12:
Get the Right Team

You can achieve success through a good plan, hard work, determination, and follow-through. However, if you want to maximize your success, it requires a team effort. Everyone who wants to do something extraordinary in life should have a solid team. This is your inner circle of people who help keep you on track to achieving your dreams. For this team, you need a coach, a mentor, a sponsor, and a cheerleader, and you need to know the difference between each of them.

Your coach is a person who knows you the best and can provide you with candid advice about how to conduct yourself. This is the sounding board you can be most open with, and air out all of your dirty laundry. They know your vices, your shortcomings, and your history. So there is never a need to put on a front when you are around your coach.

Much like an athlete has multiple coaches for different situations and stages of their career, you will have multiple coaches. All of my real friends are also my coaches. Still, none of them are able to coach me on every aspect of my life. For example, the person I go to for dating advice isn't the same person I go to for advice on dealing with my boss.

Know your coaches' limitations. Floyd Mayweather, Jr. wouldn't get a coach who has never worn boxing gloves to train him for a fight. Similarly, you should not get a coach who has never held a job to give you work-related advice. Nor should you allow your most short tempered and confrontational friend to give you advice on deescalating a conflict.

This is a good time to point out that if you don't have friends who can coach you on some aspect of your life, you should probably get new friends. Back home we have a saying, "Don't be the biggest fish in a little pond." It can be a comfortable feeling to be better than all of your friends at everything (i.e. the biggest fish). These are situations where you are always the best on your team, you always know you are going to win, and/or everyone always defers to you. However, remember our discussion on discomfort. You have to leave your comfort zone to maximize your growth. Having nobody to challenge you means you have nobody that can push you to grow. Though it is comfortable, you will slow your progression towards your goals and stunt your personal growth.

Don't be the biggest fish in a little pond. Surround yourself with talented people who can challenge you to improve. Any person that I call "friend" is better than me at something. There is some aspect of my spiritual, personal or professional development that they can guide me

126

through. If someone does not possess that ability then it is likely that the friendship is a toxic relationship. It has been my experience that these types of toxic relationships will make it more difficult for you to achieve your dreams.

In a work environment, your mentor is a person who is or has been where you are going. As such, this person can, and will, help you navigate the pitfalls you will encounter in your professional life. All coaches with relevant work experience can be mentors, but MOST MENTORS SHOULD NOT BE COACHES. It is a huge mistake to approach your mentor with things that can be categorized as petty or overly personal. Your mentor does not need to know how much you hate your supervisor, or hear your extensive ranting about your annoying in-laws.

That is not to say that you cannot have personal conversations with your mentor. Having general conversations about your family, or a shared interest is completely acceptable. Additionally, it is important to find someone you can have candid conversations with about difficult professional questions like:

How to best navigate starting a family with your work responsibilities, how to broach the subject of working remotely to better handle family health issues, or when is it an appropriate time to report the inappropriate behavior of a supervisor to their supervisor, etc.

You never want to engage in angry ranting or perpetually complain (especially about personal matters) to your mentors. This is disrespectful of their time, and you risk being perceived as a nuisance to be ignored rather than a protégé to be guided.

> "Associate with men of good quality if you esteem your own reputation; for it is better to be alone than in bad company"
> Pres. George Washington

Additionally, do not go to your mentor for advice you really don't want. I myself have been guilty of going to friends for "advice," when I really just want them to affirm the course of action that I already plan to do. This practice can be acceptable with friends, and even coaches, but it is not acceptable with your mentor. If your mentor strongly recommends that you do or don't do something, and you ignore that recommendation, then you may make a lasting negative impression on them. This kind of impression is something that you may never be able to recover from. That does not mean that you have to treat everything your mentor says as the gospel truth, or that you can't go against their recommendations for valid reasons. Still, if it becomes clear to your mentor that you made a decision before asking for advice and no logic is going to sway you, then they will feel like you are wasting their time.

Your sponsor is the person with access that can open doors for you. When I say "access," what do I mean? The first thing you may think of is money and other tangible resources. Wealth does give you "access," but I would define the term more broadly. Access is the ability to be heard and listened to by people with relevant decision-making authority. Thus, even though things like money can help someone get access, your sponsor does not actually need money to have access.

To illustrate this explanation consider the president/CEO of a Fortune 500 company and the sitting President of the United States. If you could only pick one of them to help you get your dream job, who would it be? Even though most company presidents and CEOs make significantly more money than the majority of the United States' past presidents, the President of the United States has far more access. One phone call from the President of the United States could get you an audience with almost any major decision maker in the world.

For your sponsor, you want someone who has both access and a willingness to use their access to help you achieve your goals and dreams. Your sponsor is a person who can get you major opportunities that you would not otherwise be considered for. You want a sponsor who is actually willing to make those kinds of calls on your behalf.

A sponsor is typically the most difficult to find because there are so few people with access. You can have multiple coaches and mentors, and you will continuously find more of them as you advance through life. Yet, most people only get a couple of opportunities to have a true sponsor. Therefore, if you find a sponsor that is willing to take you under their wing, foster that relationship.

Fostering a relationship with a sponsor is a very different experience. Typically, these are people who have very limited time. So you should have very concise updates when you meet with them. On most occasions, before any planned meeting with my sponsor, I meet with one of my coaches and one of my mentors to refine what I want to talk about. You could sometimes only see your sponsor once or twice a year, so it is important to make a good impression and use your time productively.

More importantly, do not treat your sponsor like a mentor. They are not the people who are supposed to help you with daily or even monthly problems. If you are going to ask your sponsor for help, it should be for a major issue or significant ask. For example, if you are trying to figure out how to deal with your annoying boss, that is a question for your mentor. If you are having difficulty securing an interview for a prestigious position at a new company, that is a conversation for your sponsor.

Navigating the process of growing your team can be difficult. I have made numerous mistakes when trying to foster relationships with potential team members. I told you earlier about losing a potential sponsor at a law firm because I did not do enough to grow that relationship. I have also lost mentors and coaches because of shortcomings in my relationship management. It is a learning process, so don't get discouraged if you have a few setbacks. Just always learn from your mistakes and do better if ever you are presented with a similar circumstance.

Ultimately, the objective of your interactions is to maintain and grow your relationship capital. Relationship capital is an intangible asset, which is a reflection of how much goodwill you have built up in a particular relationship. The amount of goodwill or relationship capital that you maintain is important because it determines how much someone is willing to do on your behalf. The more relationship capital you have in a relationship, the more someone is willing to do for you. However, anytime someone does something for you, you spend some of your relationship capital.

How do you build relationship capital? There are numerous ways to build your relationship capital with someone. Helping them when they are in need, delivering on your promises, showing respect, being reliable, showing concern, and generally anything that endears you to someone or improves your reputation in their eyes. This could be as big as saving someone in a tough situation or as small as remembering someone's birthday. Even being from the same alma mater or apart of the same fraternity/sorority can be a way to develop a rapport and increase your relationship capital with someone.

It is, however, important to realize that your relationship capital is a limited resource that can run out. If you are constantly asking for something and never reciprocating in any way, your relationship will become "bankrupt." In which case, you will lose your relationship with that person. Once destroyed, a relationship is extremely hard to redevelop. So make sure that you utilize your team efficiently, and above all else, don't waste people's time! Wasting someone's time is often the quickest way to bankrupt your relationship with them.

There is one more person that I think every team should have. This person is your personal cheerleader. As the title implies, they are in your life to spur you to success. This person may not be good for advice and may have no idea what it takes for you to accomplish your goals. However, regardless of what you do in life, they are there with a kind and uplifting word. These are the people who most relish in your success and consistently cheer you through your setbacks.

Do not mistake a fan for a cheerleader. When you start accomplishing more of your goals and working your way towards your dream, you are going to catch some people's attention. You may have some people noticing your success and congratulating you. These are not your cheerleaders these are your fans. Cheerleaders do not just pat you on the back when you are doing well; they also continue to be a positive encouraging force when things are going bad. That is what differentiates a fan from a cheerleader, and you want the latter on your team and not the former.

Why is this distinction important? Have you ever sat through a game that was a clear blowout from the beginning? I had the great misfortune of going to one of the smallest Division 1 universities in the country and the smallest Division 1 football school in Texas (Rice University). What that means is our small school, with less than 40,000 alumni living and dead, plays against some of the best nationally ranked football teams in the nation. Some of these teams represent universities with more than 50,000 students on campus each year. Our football defeats are so well documented that when President John F. Kennedy announced the national effort to put a man on the moon, he equated the seemingly impossible task of putting a man on the moon to Rice University playing the

University of Texas in football on a yearly basis. As such, I have watched my team take some astronomical defeats on the gridiron.

What normally happens when a team starts losing badly? The fans stop cheering and start leaving. Have you ever seen a cheerleader leave the field while the game was still in progress? No matter how horrible the blowout is, the cheerleaders keep cheering in a seemingly forlorn hope that their team will recover. And every so often they do!

Similarly, when things are going badly for you, you need cheerleaders in your corner who will not abandon you when you are down. These are the people who will hope against hope and still lift your spirits in the face of almost certain defeat. This is important because, no matter how self-motivated and independent you are, it is hard to keep fighting, what feels like, a losing battle. Much like the effective rewards system discussed earlier in this book, a cheerleader can keep you motivated to work even when the outcome seems bleak. In doing so, a good cheerleader can help you snatch success from the jaws of defeat.

Another important function of a cheerleader is to help you refocus after a setback. No matter how good you are at what you do, you are going to make a mistake. Whether it is in your professional life, personal life, or academic life, there will be times where you do something you consider "bone-headed" or "idiotic." The problem with those types of mistakes is that we have a tendency to fixate on them. In doing so, we can slip into a rut and start making more mistakes. Your cheerleader is the one who is going to get you to refocus after those bone-headed mistakes.

For me, my greatest cheerleader is my oldest brother Jamar. I can go to my Mom for mentoring, and my brother Ray for coaching, but in those situations where I just need to be cheered up, Jamar is my go-to-guy. Whether it was a bad breakup, a crappy boss, a major mistake on an assignment or a bad grade, he has always been the eternal optimist who consistently cheers me up and cheers me on. No matter what endeavor I undertake, he is the person I most count on to give me the unyielding moral support that I need to get back to working towards my goals.

Deciding who will be on your team can have a profound impact on your life. These are the people who will guide you through your personal, spiritual, academic and professional journey. Thus, the people on your team will influence your success and the person you become. Some of these influences may start off subtle. However, over time, the team you surround yourself with can drastically alter your life trajectory for better or for worse.

> "You can't hang out with chickens and expect to soar with eagles."
> Joel Osteen

Because association breeds assimilation, who you surround yourself with will tell people a lot about you. "Birds of a feather flock together." It is assumed that you share the characteristics of the people that you flock towards. If you associate with people who are not doing anything with their lives or considered untrustworthy, people will assume that you are the same. Conversely, if your team is filled with good, ambitious, and dedicated members, then people will assume you have good character and are ambitious and dedicated.

Choose your team wisely!

Chapter 13:
Learn From Mistakes: Yours & Others

Mistakes are not the enemy of success, repeating them is! Anyone who has done anything worthwhile has encountered setbacks, made mistakes, and/or regretted past decisions. Making mistakes does not stop you from being successful. As long as you learn from your mistakes and don't dwell on them, mistakes can be an invaluable part of success.

Governor Ann Richards said it best. "…we all have to learn from our mistakes, and we learn from those mistakes a lot more than we learn from the things we succeeded in doing." When you succeed, you have only used your previous knowledge to identify a way to achieve success.

Additionally, you are less likely to critically assess your performance or actions in circumstances that result in your success. Therefore, the only thing you glean from successful situations is that your approach worked in that circumstance.

> "Success is a lousy teacher. It seduces smart people into thinking they can't lose."
> Bill Gates

Making a mistake is different. First and foremost, you are far more likely to analyze your overall performance when you make a mistake. Furthermore, if you are wise, you will do everything in your power to make sure that you never make that mistake again.

For most of us, learning from our own mistakes is self-evident and not a particularly revolutionary idea. However, when you are trying to achieve an ambitious dream, learning from your own mistakes cannot be the only way that you learn. There are some mistakes you cannot afford to make because they are both figuratively and literally fatal. As such, there are some lessons you need to learn through the experiences of others.

"A hard head makes a soft behind." This quote has been a warning to children throughout the south for generations. If you had the great misfortune of hearing this uttered from your mother, grandmother, aunts or any adult, it meant that you were very close to getting a spanking. What does this have to do with you achieving success?

The reason the statement begins with "A hard head," is because it was only used when you were given instructions that you ignored. When you ignored the warnings of your elders, you were inviting calamity in the form of a belt across your backside. Failing to heed the instructions or warnings of those who came before you can, often time, result in unnecessary harm. This is the same logic that gave rise to the statement "Those who do not learn from history are doomed to repeat it."

Time is the only resource in life that you need for every accomplishment and that you cannot replenish once you lose it. If you want to maximize your success and achieve lofty dreams in your lifetime, you do not have the time to repeat mistakes. Put bluntly, if you want to accomplish any dream worthwhile, you cannot waste time unnecessarily duplicating mistakes. Though life is a great teacher, it is far more time efficient when you learn your lessons in a proactive manner. This means that not only should you learn from your own mistakes and try never to repeat the same one, but you should also learn from the mistakes of others so that you do not repeat those either.

> "See or make a mistake once and it becomes a lesson; afterwards, make that same mistake and it becomes a choice."

How do you effectively learn from the mistakes of others?

Do your homework. There is a surprising amount of literature out there about navigating everything from raising a child to starting a business. Often there is plenty of published material, instructional videos, and readily available information about the goal you are pursuing. Whether it is a seminar, watching online instructional videos, or reading a book on the subject matter, you should be willing to consume all the available information about what you are trying to accomplish.

Additionally, sometimes the simplest way to get inside information about the route you are taking is to ask the people that have already been there. Even when you are doing something that is considered novel, there will be aspects of your journey that resemble or are identical to other people's journey. I have never met another person who has a B.S. in engineering, a J.D. and a Ph.D. in engineering, and I have never heard of anyone getting all three degrees before turning 26 years old. Thus, there was no one person who could advise me on every potential pitfall of my journey. However, I know plenty of people with a B.S. in engineering. I know three lawyers in my family. Additionally, once my mom got her Ph.D. in engineering, I had an in-house resource to help navigate the pitfalls of a Ph.D. program. So, at each stage of my journey, I found somebody who accomplished that segment of my journey.

Find someone who has achieved or attempted to achieve a dream or goal that you want to achieve. Then ask them about their journey.

"What are some things you wish you had known when you began your journey?" "If you had it to do again what would you do differently?" "What would you do the same?" "What are your regrets?" "What was the most helpful and the most harmful to you achieving your goal?" "Do you have any recommendations for me?"

You may be surprised by the people who will take time out of their schedule to tell you about themselves. Remember, if all that you have to fear is them saying "No," go for it! The potential benefit that you could gain from their years of experience greatly outweighs the downside of potentially hearing the word "No."

It is worth noting that I have never been turned down for a conversation with someone when I ask them about their personal journey. In my experience that people feel flattered and want to share when someone is genuinely interested in them. I might have had to be persistent if they were busy, but ultimately the people I reached out to felt excited to provide guidance.

Notice that I suggested talking to both people who achieved and *attempted to achieve* one of your goals or dreams. We often times ignore people who we do not perceive as being successful enough. In general, that is a huge mistake, but it is especially a mistake when you are trying to learn from others. In the south, we have a saying, "A broken clock is right two times a day." This is a colloquialism that tells us you can learn something from everyone; regardless of how seemingly "broken" they are, everyone has some nuggets of wisdom to share. Be open to receiving good advice from unexpected sources.

> "Sometimes the road less traveled is less traveled for a reason"
> Jerry Seinfeld

Additionally, there is just as much value in learning what not to do as there is in learning what to do. Let's say you want to start a business and you know someone who ran an otherwise successful business that failed because of not keeping good tax records. This person can give you great advice on avoiding mistakes like failing to keep track of vendor expenses or improper withholdings. Similarly, some of the best advice I got for succeeding in college came from people who flunked out. Those were the people who told me to keep partying to a minimum, don't skip class, get your books before classes start, and gave me several other tips for success in college.

Remember that learning what paths not to go down can be very helpful in locating your best route to success. Not only can you learn this lesson from people who have been down those "wrong paths," you can learn from people who avoided those paths altogether. "Sometimes the road less traveled is less traveled for a reason." (Jerry Seinfeld) Understanding, why people chose to avoid certain paths in life can inform your decisions.

There are, often times, more paths to failure than there are to success. So don't feel the need to blindly stumble through the plethora of paths laid out before you. Use the wise counsel and example set by others to avoid mistakes and identify your optimal paths to success.

Chapter 14:
Don't Share Your Dream with Everyone

I grew up in church. I was sometimes there four or five times a week. This was especially true after my dad passed. The church was a convenient source of free babysitting and positive male role models. Whether or not you are Christian, you cannot deny the fact that the Bible is an incredibly intriguing read that has something for everyone. I personally love the stories, especially the ones from the Old Testament.

The Bible is full of stories that you can derive life lessons from. I learned to be fearless from the story of Daniel (Daniel 6:1-21), Shadrach, Meshach and Abednego (Daniel 3:1-30). From Joshua, I learned that asking for the

Moon and the Stars isn't an unreasonable expectation from life (Joshua 10:12-13). The story of David taught me that no matter how Godly you are (Acts 13:22) you can make mistakes (2 Samuel 11:1-27). The primary lesson from this chapter is also something that you can learn from the Bible, and that lesson is, "Don't share your dream with everyone."

This comes from one of my favorite Biblical stories, the story of Joseph in Genesis (Chapter 37-45). Joseph is sometimes called "The Dreamer." Through his dreams and interpretations of dreams, he saved his family and an entire nation of people from starvation.

Joseph was the 11th of 12 brothers, yet he was his father's favorite son. His brothers resented him for this favoritism. Not having very high situational awareness, he compounded their agitation towards him by sharing his dream with them. In his dream, he lorded over them and all eleven of his brothers bowed at his feet.

This was especially problematic because, under the rules of their society, the eldest brother was supposed to be the leader. In an effort to prevent his dream from coming to pass, his brothers sold him into slavery and faked his death. Ultimately, after years of triumph and misfortune, Joseph used his gift for interpreting dreams and his acquired skills of managing estates to work his way from being a slave and prisoner to the second most powerful man in Egypt next to Pharaoh himself.

Eventually, his dream did come to pass, and his brothers bowed at his feet. Still, because he openly shared his dream, the route he took to get to his destination involved several pitfalls. Treat this story as a cautionary tale. Had Joseph not so liberally shared his dream, he may not have angered his brothers and gotten sold into slavery.

You might ask, "Wasn't being a slave a necessary part of his journey?" While struggle can definitely be a character building experience, Joseph's journey through slavery and prison might not have been a necessary hardship. Joseph becomes the second most powerful man in Egypt by correctly interpreting a dream that haunted Pharaoh. His interpretation of the dream saved Egypt and some surrounding areas from desolation at the hands of a horrible famine. It is quite possible that he could have gotten to interpret that dream and get that same position even without the hardship of his slavery and imprisonment.

Thus, the lessons that I want you to take from this story, is twofold. 1) Remember that your past tragedy does not dictate your future trajectory, and 2) You should not share your dream with everyone.

Your tragedy does not dictate your trajectory! Anyone who has heard me give a speech has probably heard me say this phrase. It is a point I reiterate every chance I get because learning this lesson was vital to my success. What does the phrase mean?

First and foremost it means that where you start does not determine where you will finish. In life, having a rocky start to your journey or a difficult past does not stop you from accomplishing great things. A lot of people think that you must have a pristine upbringing without heartache and hardship to succeed in life. That is just not true! Some of the greatest success stories in the world start from humble, or even tragic, beginnings.

Additionally, the phrase is meant to convey that: *You are not the sum total of your circumstances; you are the sum total of your choices.* You are not defined by the circumstances you were born into, or what happens to you in life. You are defined by how you choose to respond to those events. Prof. Randy Pausch said it best, "We cannot change the cards we are dealt, just how we play the hand."

Do you feel that you have been dealt a horrible hand in life? That may be true. Now what? It is still your responsibility to make the best use of what you are given in life. In the story of Joseph, he rose from being a slave and an ex-convict to the second most powerful man in a foreign country. There are contemporary stories of people defying the odds every day.

Do not fall into the trap of statistics. As in, "statistics say that growing up in a low-income household makes you X times more likely to go to jail."

Or, "Statistics show that people with your condition have less than an X % chance of surviving."

Or even, "Statistics show that people from your town have an X in 1,000 chance of graduating with a college degree."

There are statistics to say that the average height of an NBA player is about 6'7. The likelihood of being drafted if you are less than 6 feet tall is slim to none. However, Muggsy Bogues was only 5'3 and drafted 12th overall in the 1987 NBA draft. He went on to have a 14-year-career in the NBA.

> "It always seems impossible until it's done"
> Nelson Mandela

You live in a world where a deafblind woman became a Harvard lawyer and world-renowned speaker, and a man with no legs ran in the Olympics. When Neil Armstrong was born nobody had ever flown more than 8 ½ miles off the surface of the planet. Less than 30 years later, he flew over 230,000 miles above the Earth's surface to the moon. Before accomplishing these feats, how many statistics and people do you think said that they were impossible?

Don't let yourself be limited by what others say is possible or likely. Things that were once impossible happen on a daily basis.

The primary lesson that the story of Joseph taught me, which is the title of the chapter, is: *Don't share your dreams with everyone.* Do not be the person who has your trajectory derailed because you shared your dreams or goals with the wrong person. How do you tell the difference between who you should and shouldn't tell your dreams to?

Ultimately, if the person isn't someone who can help you progress towards a goal or a dream they don't really need to know about them. This was a lesson that I wish I had learned sooner because I had a nasty habit of telling people too much information. Though not as extreme, I have definitely experienced the Joseph effect of telling the wrong person my future plans and turning what could have been a helpful ally into a saboteur.

Let me give you a more contemporary example of how this can play out to your detriment. My first time working for a technical company was a leading medical device company. Even though this was after my fourth year in college, this was the first summer I could get a job working for a major company. Up until that point, I was under the age of 18, and companies would not hire me because of child labor laws. I was excited to be applying my engineering skillset in the "real world," and took on as many projects as I could. Though my technical skillset was on pair with people 3-5 years older than me, I still had a lot to learn when it came to interpersonal skills.

One day my supervisor asked me, "Where do you see yourself in 5 - 10 years?"

The question caught me off guard since it seemingly came out of the blue. I said the first thing that came to mind. It was something along the lines of "I like being able to manage hands-on projects, and I like the position that you are in because you are close enough to the ground to get to do some interesting stuff. So I think I would like to be in a position like yours."

> Mistakes are not the enemy of success, repeating them is!

I, being the naïve 18-year-old that I was at the time, didn't realize how that response was interpreted. What my manager heard was "I want your job, and even though it took you 20 years to get here, I think I will be able to do it in 5 years."

Needless to say, our working relationship became far less friendly after that point. Since I didn't realize what I had done, it took me a while to realize that I was being sabotaged. Suddenly he became more critical of everything I did. One week I was communicating too little, the next week I was communicating too much. I would do something extremely well for an intern, but he would evaluate me against the fulltime employees he had been working with for a decade or more. He skipped meetings with me, and "forgot" to send me information for my projects. Any way that he could delay me he did.

Seemingly overnight, that went from the best job I had ever had to the most difficult. I had to dedicate a significant amount of time to finding ways to work around him. Because of sharing a goal I should have kept to myself, my manager went from a very helpful ally to a continual roadblock.

Now, his attempts at sabotage did not absolve me from achieving my goals for that employment opportunity. I had to keep my objectives in mind, which were to complete all of my projects, exceed expectations, and leave a positive impression of myself. Despite the continuous hindrance, I recognize that my success is my priority. So even though it meant some extra work, and spending extra time meeting with and updating his supervisors of my progress, I did what was necessary to make sure that I achieved my goals.

Nevertheless, my journey would have been easier if I didn't share my dreams and goals with potential saboteurs. Put more simply, don't go out of your way to give haters additional reasons to hate. Although it is not always easy to identify somebody who is going to be one of your haters, there are a couple of principles that can help.

How do you identify people that you shouldn't tell your dreams to? Going back to our previous section; identify your sponsors, coaches, mentors and cheerleaders. If a person doesn't fall into one of those categories or have the potential to fall into one of those categories, they don't need to know what you are planning until it is done. In other words, the only people that need to know your dreams are the people who have the ability to help you achieve them.

Now just because somebody falls into one of the four categories, doesn't mean that they need to know everything that you are planning. Be careful whenever you are directly or inadvertently telling somebody that you are expecting to do something faster or better than them. Think about my experience with my manager. If the person is secure in themselves, they won't mind, but a lot of people can take that as a challenge. I learned from the mistake I made in telling him that I was going to get the same job he currently had in far less time. When it came time to talk to my Ph.D. advisors, I knew I wanted to get a Ph.D. in three years, but I did not tell that to any of my advisors until after I was approved for graduation.

Don't give people additional reasons to "hate on you" or be unnecessarily competitive with you. This is an especially good principle in circumstances where the person already looks down on you. Although it is unfortunate, we all have a pretty good idea of the people that think of themselves as being above others. If possible, you really should avoid having these types of people in your inner circle, to begin with. However, sometimes it is unavoidable. When you have a person like this as a member of your team, keep information exchange with them on a need to know basis.

When you are pursuing aggressive goals, you will occasionally rub some people the wrong way. You may hear things like:

"Who do you think you are?"
"You're not better than me!"
"That's impossible!"
"You're dreaming!" etc.

And maybe some people might even go out of their way to derail your progress. This sabotage and discouragement may even come from some people who you trust or love.

Do not let this discourage you!

The important thing to remember is that regardless of what others do, or say, you are responsible for your own success. And if you are like me and Joseph and accidentally let your mouth earn you some extra stumbling blocks, do not be discouraged! Go over them, around them, under them, or through them, but get to your dream.

"I was once considered just a dreamer, but I paid my dues and turned so many doubters to believers"
Justin 'Big K.R.I.T.' Scott

Chapter 15:
Every Ending is a New Beginning

If you are aggressive, thoughtful, and consistent in striving towards a goal, chances are, you will eventually achieve it! The chapters up until now have given you the tools you need to set and pursue goals effectively. I am confident that if you use the planning techniques, exercises, and methods outlined in this book, you will accomplish great things. Once you accomplish those goals, what's next?

My encouragement is that you set a new and challenging goal for yourself. I am a firm believer that having something to strive for and work towards is essential for a long, joyous life. I wish I could take credit for that nugget of wisdom, but it actually came from my Great Aunt Dimple Naomi Mims Davis. She lived to be 94 years old, and could figuratively, and in some cases literally, run circles around people 30 and 40 years her junior. Even in her 90s, she was known for throwing on her shades and cruising around Oklahoma City with the top dropped on her convertible.

As you can imagine, many people wanted to know the secret to how she remained so energetic. Her answer was simple, she stayed busy. Although I don't think the word busy quite explains her mantra. I remember visiting her on one occasion; keep in mind that she was between 88 and 90 years old at this point, and I was only 16 or 17 at the time. In my mind, I was going to do so many helpful things around her house; the reality was that I barely got to wash a dish the entire time I was with her.

Anytime she was awake she was moving (cooking, cleaning, organizing, preparing for a church event, etc.). She was a cosmetologist by trade, and at 90 years old she still did manicures and pedicures for a few customers she kept after retiring. Additionally, I could take up half of a chapter listing the ministries in which she either led or was an active participant. I am convinced that I could publish an entire book on the people's lives that she impacted.

With the exception of the few cat naps she would take and the times she would indulge in watching the latest Tyler Perry play on her TV, there were not many times in a 24 hour period when she wasn't trying to do something. In general, whenever she finished a phase of her life she readily picked up a new mission.

That does not mean work 24/7 until your dying day. Although she was busy, she was having fun! I know that working with church ministries and attending national church conventions might not be your definition of a good time, but she got joy out of it. Her philosophy was "Do all the good you can, to all the people you can, just as long as you can." Helping people and fellowshipping at her church gave her fulfillment and great joy.

So when you find yourself at a stage of life where you have accomplished everything you want to do professionally, setting new goals might be some personal goals. If you like to travel, maybe you will make it your mission to visit all 50 states. If family brings you joy, you could make it your mission to mentor the young people in your family. Or you could be like my Aunt Dimple and just take joy in the happiness of other people and decide to "Do all the good you can, to all the people you can, just as long as you can!"

Honestly, if you get to be like Aunt Dimple and continuously know what your next mission in life is going to be, it is a great feeling. When you never have to ask "what's next," and just move from one mission/goal to the next one seamlessly, accomplishing your goals is a completely joyous experience. And that is the way I had been after accomplishing every major milestone before now.

However, when I graduated this last time, I had to ask myself "what's next?" That question can be a simple but daunting conundrum. Using myself as an example; I spent almost two decades pursuing a single dream. Every significant stride and accomplishment I have made in my life has been a progression towards that dream. Up until this point in my life, there had never been a time where I didn't know what the next step was. Truthfully, there were very few times in the past 20 years where I didn't know exactly what I would be doing in 3 months – 6 months. There was always a new class, new extracurricular activity, new internship, or new school that was just over the horizon. And, with the exception of choosing between universities or jobs, I never had to question what was next.

> *"Do all the good you can, to all the people you can, just as long as you can!"*
> Dimple Davis

What was even more reassuring about that lifestyle was that I never really had to question my ability to succeed. After 11 years of college, and almost 23 years of school in general, I no longer had to question my ability to succeed in school. Sure there were tests I wasn't confident about or subjects that I struggled with, but on the whole, I know how to prepare for a final exam, take a test and/or write a paper. Thus, the experience of being in school was comfortable and known.

Furthermore, being very honest, I grew accustomed to being praised. After 20+ years of school, I knew how to do praiseworthy things in the classroom. To an extent, though I acquired a lot of work and extracurricular experience along the way, my most praised and praiseworthy accomplishments were accomplished in the classroom.

I share this to underscore the anxiety and fear of moving into the next phase of life. Regardless of what I choose to do next, the phase of my life with final exams, graduations, and graduation parties is over. On August 17th when all the celebrations had ended, and the graduation balloons had deflated and fallen to the ground, I was left with the question of "What's next?"

Note that after every graduation and every milestone in my life I had been asked that question. "Now that you have done X, what's next?" In one form or another, I had heard that question for over a decade from other people. Yet, what was uncomfortable, shocking, anxiety-causing, and flat out terrifying was that after over a decade of being asked that question, for the first time I said, "I don't know…" Thus this became the first time I ever had to ask myself "What is next?"

For some of you reading this, you may have reacted to those last paragraphs with bewilderment. You may be saying, "How could you be terrified after positioning yourself to do whatever you want?" That is a good thing. That likely means, that like my Aunt Dimple, you have generally progressed from one challenge to the next without much interruption. It is my sincere hope that, whenever you accomplish your goals, your reaction is excitement, celebration, and an immediate resolve to progress to the next challenge.

However, if you find yourself having dedicated a significant portion of your life to a goal or a dream that you are no longer pursuing and feel haunted by the uncertainty you now face, this chapter was written specifically for you. The wording of the previous sentence is intentional. You may not have come to this uncertain "what's next" phase because you accomplished everything you wanted to accomplish in the previous phase of life. And that is ok; this chapter is also for you.

I cannot unequivocally tell you how to get past this uncomfortable stage of your journey. Still, I can tell you what worked for me. In the months following this last graduation, I did four things 1) Remind & Realize 2) Recharge 3) Re-engage and 4) Repeat.

5 R's of Restarting
REMIND
REALIZE
RECHARGE
RE-ENGAGE
REPEAT

First and foremost, the easiest thing to do when you are standing at the precipice of a new journey is to get discouraged. You start questioning whether you can succeed in this new phase of life. You can easily get down on yourself and really start to let fear and anxiety take a hold of you. In those moments you want to "Remind."

Remind yourself of where you started from and how far that you have come! Have you ever noticed that fitness programs always make you take pictures of yourself when you start? My reaction had always been: *what's the point of this; I am not going to show this to anyone else and I am not going to forget what I look like*. I realized that that was actually false. While in law school I had gotten a bit more than a little chubby, and started slimming down after I graduated and came back to Texas. Recently, I looked at an old picture of myself and was astonished that I looked so different.

Contrary to my belief, it is very easy to forget who you used to be. Growth is such a gradual process, that you can easily ignore it when it is happening. In your mind, you are only comparing yourself to the way you were yesterday or an hour ago, and on that time horizon, not much change occurs. But after months and years of progressing towards a goal, you will become a completely new person! Make the conscious effort to see that comparison, and remind yourself how far you have come.

Think about every milestone you have passed. Think about every interim goal you have achieved. Look at some of the old pictures of yourself, and look at some of the old writing and work you have produced. The more of that you do, the more you will internalize how much you have done.

At some point, let that reminder grow into a realization. Realize that the person that was able to accomplish all of those achievements has more that they can do! Let that realization sink in and tell yourself, "I am just getting started!"

Once you "Remind" yourself of who you were and "Realize" how exceptional your transformation has been, it is time to "Relax." In my experience, the best way to do this is to have some fun! I don't care how you feel, you need to celebrate! Revisit the chapter on celebrating your victories, and do that here. Even if the last chapter of your life didn't end the way you wanted it to, you need to do something legitimately fun to celebrate that last phase closing. At the point that you have reminded yourself of how far you have come, you should have plenty to celebrate. However, if you feel like you don't have anything to celebrate, celebrate the fact that you are alive today; whereas, there are thousands of people who didn't make it through yesterday. Another day is another opportunity. That alone is something to be celebrated!

It is important for you to celebrate because you have worked hard and inherently accumulated stress that you are probably unaware of. It could be in the forms of both mental and physical stress. If you have been pursuing your goals relentlessly, your body and mind might be locked in a perpetual state of "tension" ready to go to work.

This tension and the resulting readiness can be useful when you have a clear objective to pursue. However, it can also stifle your ability to think. The fun that you have will give you a chance to relax that tension and make you better able to think about what the next phase of your life will look like.

"Celebration" doesn't just mean party; for most people parties are not actually relaxing and become an additional source of stress. After this last graduation, yes I had celebration parties, but that was not how I celebrated the milestone. Parties stress me out and they feel like a waste of money to me. Thus, to an extent, parties increase my tension rather than relieving it.

My actual celebration was traveling and visiting friends and family. I literally flew from coast to coast and took road trips all around Texas. In fact, I cranked out a large portion of this book while sitting seaside visiting my friend in Bermuda, and I finished the first draft of it while attending a wedding in Las Vegas.

Make sure that your celebration is what you enjoy doing, and not what you feel like you have to do. Whenever you say "celebrate," don't automatically think party or travel. There are so many interesting activities and such a variety of people out there that everybody's celebration can't possibly look the same. Whether it is going fishing, checking an item off of your bucket list, going to your favorite sporting events, doing the NASCAR racing experience, or golfing, do what makes you happy, and do it to the fullest!

I spent the majority of my trip to Bermuda doing 2-a-day workouts with my friend who is a former national heptathlete. That was fun for me, but as far as most people are concerned that was a horrible way to enjoy an island paradise. You are "supposed to" sunbathe, hang out at beaches, go to parties, and drink the night away. None of those things sound fun or relaxing to me. However, working out and ending the day with Netflix marathons and writing was exceptionally relaxing to me.

There is no right or wrong answer for how you should celebrate as long as you do something. I do not recommend sitting around your house staring at the ceiling. If you don't want to leave the house, do an indoor activity. Read some books, build some things, play some games that you thoroughly enjoy, or basically do anything that will keep you from being idle with your thoughts. There is nothing more annoying than being stuck with your thoughts or inactive when you are in the midst of uncertainty.

Next, you must "Re-engage," pursuing a goal. I do not mean another dream or major milestone goal. At this point, just find something to do that challenges you.

This may unfold naturally while you are celebrating. While you are trying to celebrate, you may find yourself drawn to certain activities, and those activities turn into interim goals. Examples of this could be getting in better shape for people who celebrate with working out, repairing your house for people who like do-it-yourself projects or even writing a book for people like me who like to write.

Additionally, based on your previous experiences, you may have people approach you with projects to work on. Examples of this could be leaders in organizations that you are affiliated with asking you for help. Or even former or current colleagues requesting your assistance with work related projects. Get involved in these opportunities.

Ultimately it is your responsibility to find something to re-engage with. If it does not occur naturally during or at the termination of your celebration, find something to do. If you can't think of anything, consider working on a cause that resonates with you. Remember this does not need to be a major milestone, just something that you can work towards and feel accomplished when completing it.

The reason that this is important is that it helps to keep you out of a rut. When you are not pursuing a goal it is easy to fall into a rut. What do I mean by a rut? It is the cycle of negative feelings towards yourself that can cause you to be unproductive but is hard to change. The way it tends to work is that you start feeling like you are wasting your days away and get down on yourself. Being down on yourself causes you to have less energy and do less with your days. As a result, you feel worse and the cycle continues. Break this cycle and/or prevent it from starting by picking a goal to pursue in the interim.

Additionally, although it shouldn't matter what other people think, most of us are not completely immune to caring. As such, it may bother us to be asked "what are you up to," and your answer is "nothing." Re-engaging gives you something to talk about in those circumstances, which in turn, makes you less likely to fall into a rut.

> "During your life, never stop dreaming. No one can take away your dreams."
> Tupac Shakur

The final step is to return to the first chapter of this book and Repeat the process of establishing and aggressively pursuing new dreams. There is no need to reinvent the wheel. You can go through the same process you used to figure out your last dream to create a new one.

I will add one piece of advice. During the re-engaging process, did you find yourself invariably drawn to a particular activity that you thoroughly enjoyed? If so, consider that that activity might make the basis for a new dream. There are people who make careers doing everything from buying clothes to traveling the world. So whatever your passion is, there is a way to succeed doing it.

Going forward, the important thing to realize is that every ending is a new beginning. Whenever you close one chapter of your life, you are automatically opening a new chapter. Don't ever let yourself get caught up in your past mistakes or past triumphs. Doing so can make you miss the exceptional moments of the present and leave you unprepared to face the future.

Chapter 16:
Be Respectful, Be Passionate and Be Thankful!

"Your attitude determines your altitude [in life]." My mom used this phrase all of the time. It was her way of saying, regardless of how intelligent or talented I was, the single greatest determinate of my success in life would be my attitude and how I treated others. Thus, there were three simple rules that I had to abide by: Be Respectful, Be Passionate, and Be Thankful. Though a simple creed, this has been the secret to all of my success.

Be Respectful: Treat everyone you meet with respect and dignity. When I say everyone, I mean everyone. People tend to find this the most difficult when they are dealing with someone they deem as "unimportant" or someone who has wronged them.

> "We all require and want respect, man or woman, black or white. It's our basic human right."
> Aretha Franklin

It is a grave mistake to pass judgment on the importance of people. You never know the impact they may have on your life. I cannot tell you how many times I have seen people disrespect custodians and administrative assistants. This is a huge mistake! You would be surprised at the amount of facetime the people you may write off as "unimportant" get with the "important" people. When your bosses boss is burning the midnight oil, often times the custodians are the only other people in the building. Also, I learned early on that most successful people don't actually control their own schedule. I cannot tell you the number of times I got on a person's calendar at the last minute, sometimes even bumping another person from their timeslot, because I treat the administrators, assistants, and secretaries with the same respect I treat the "people in charge." Respect is something that is free to give and invaluable when returned.

Disrespecting people who wrong you is a pointless exercise that can have a negative impact on your success. Another southern idiom is, "Two wrongs don't make a right." Behaving disrespectfully is wrong, even when it is done to somebody who has harmed you. People are constantly watching and evaluating you. If a potential mentor or sponsor sees you disrespecting someone, it will not matter what the other person did. They will only see what you are doing, and will likely develop a negative opinion of your personality. Is expressing your disdain for a person you dislike worth sabotaging yourself?

Additionally, by allowing somebody to alter your temperament, you have given them control over you. You do not have to befriend people that harm you, but being able to show everyone a base level of respect is essential. By finding a way to show respect, you force yourself to let go of your animosity. When you can let go of the past it is a truly freeing experience. This is beneficial because the mental capacity that is no longer allocated to thinking of snide remarks or ways to "one-up them," can be applied to more aggressively pursuing your goals. Remember, you do not respect people for their benefit, you respect them for yours.

> "It's not an easy journey, to get to a place where you forgive people. But it is such a powerful place, because it frees you."
> Tyler Perry

Be passionate: This entire book has been about making your dreams come true. When you choose a dream to pursue, make it a dream you can be passionate about! Life is too short to pursue things that do not stir your soul.

Because my dad died when I was 10 years old I don't have the most memories of him. What I do remember was how passionate he was about fixing things. This applied to everything from cars and tractors to people and lives. Whether it was opening our home to guests so that they could get back on their feet, or getting under cars in his Sunday best after church to bring a dead car back to life, fixing things was his passion. He loved being able to take what others saw as trash, and restore them to treasures. He loved it so much that he did it whether it was his spare time or for work and whether it was for pay or for free. Seeing that, I understood that life is more complete when you are doing something that you can be that passionate about.

When you find something you can pursue with that kind of passion, pursue it!

Be Thankful: I know it is popular to talk about being "self-made." I am sure that some people will look at my history and call me "self-made." I came from a single parent household, grew up without much money, helped pay bills since I was 10 years old and moved out on my own a week after my 15th birthday. To go from that to the youngest engineer in the nation, the youngest barred attorney in the state of Texas and a Ph.D. before the age of 26 years old, I could probably be the definition of being "self-made." But ultimately there is no such thing as a self-made person.

Regardless of how much you had to do on your own, it is impossible to succeed without the help of others. It could be a parent or sibling who sacrificed so that you could afford to pursue your dreams, a person who took a risk giving you an opportunity, or someone who took time out of their day to give you some life-changing advice. Whatever the case, we all have people in our life that have helped us get to where we are and will help us get to where we want to be.

When those people spend time, money, effort, or influence to help you achieve, never forget to take the time to say "Thank You."

> "Your attitude determines your altitude"

Because I take my own advice; I want to take this time to thank all of those people who have contributed to making this book a reality. Also, thank you for reading this book, please apply the principles herein to make your dreams come true.

Acknowledgments

First and foremost thanks be to God; without Him I could not have accomplished anything that I have done, which includes writing this book. Thank you again to everyone who helped make this book a reality. Thank you to everyone who has inspired me over the years, and continues to inspire me to this day. And thank you to my personal team and my support network; you all know who you are, and you made me who I am.

Even though that covers everyone, I would be remised if I didn't make some special acknowledgments.

Thank you to my editing team for the great work they did: Dr. Tanya Dugat Wickliff (aka Mom), Semaj Fields, Brittani 'Tani' Saeun, Whitley Brock, Raymond Wickliff, and Jamar Dugat. Your input was invaluable to finishing this project. Also, thanks to the people over at Grammarly, Inc. for developing a solid proofreading program.

I want to thank Carolyn Crump of Crump Digital Designs for her work on the front and back cover. Thank you for your patience and vision.

Thank you to the beautiful country of Bermuda and my Bermudian friends for being so welcoming. I especially want to thank Andrea Jackson for opening her home to me and for not being bothered by my feverish typing at random hours of the day and night.

Las Vegas, NV will always have a special place in my heart because it was where I finished the first draft of this book. Thank you to the Waltons for allowing me to be MIA for a lot of your pre-wedding festivities.

Thank you to my mentor and friend Tavis Smiley and the Smiley Books team for all the guidance. This process would have been incredibly difficult without your support.

Thank you to Chester D.T. Baldwin for encouraging me to focus on finishing this book. I appreciate the vote of confidence, and I have not forgotten that this is only item #1 on the to-do list you gave me.

I couldn't publish my first book without acknowledging my families' hometowns – Ames, Dayton, Liberty and Raywood, and the state of Texas that I love. Whether it was getting my first car in Pflugerville, attending my first college class in Denton, driving to DFW for prom, becoming an engineer in Houston, or becoming Dr. Wickliff in Aggieland (College Station), my personal journey has been inextricably linked to Texas. For that reason, I love every corner of my state from the canyons in the Pan Handle to the beaches in the south and from the deserts out in West Texas to Liberty County in the east. I hope to one day visit every place in between!

– Cortlan –

Follow me on social media to give and get updates. I want to hear from you! Also, take a picture of yourself with this book and share it on my social media pages.

 www.**YoungAndDriven**.com

 www.Instagram.com/**YoungAndDrivenBook**

 www.Facebook.com/**YoungAndDrivenBook**

 www.Twitter.com/**YoungAndDrivenB**

For booking information:

www.CortlanWickliff.com

- or -

Cortlan.Wickliff@gmail.com

*If you are **Audacious** enough to dream, **Bold** enough to try, and **Courageous** enough to try again, then you will always be on the right track to making your dreams come true.*

42053725R00102

Made in the USA
Middletown, DE
14 April 2019